T0146383

Examining ISIS Support and Opposition Networks on Twitter

Elizabeth Bodine-Baron, Todd C. Helmus, Madeline Magnuson, Zev Winkelman

For more information on this publication, visit www.rand.org/t/RR1328

Library of Congress Cataloging-in-Publication Data is available for this publication.

ISBN: 978-0-8330-9589-3

Published by the RAND Corporation, Santa Monica, Calif.

© Copyright 2016 RAND Corporation

RAND® is a registered trademark.

Cover: Adapted from South_agency/iStock and tanuha2001/iStock.

Support RAND
Make a tax-deductible charitable contribution at
www.rand.org/giving/contribute

www.rand.org

Preface

The Islamic State in Iraq and Syria (ISIS), like no other terrorist organization before, has used Twitter and other social media channels to broadcast its message, inspire followers, and recruit new fighters. Though much less heralded, ISIS opponents have also taken to Twitter to castigate the ISIS message. This report draws on publicly available Twitter data to examine this ongoing debate about ISIS on Arabic Twitter and to better understand the networks of ISIS supporters and opponents on Twitter.

To support the countermessaging effort and to more deeply understand ISIS supporters and opponents, this study uses a mixed-methods analytic approach including lexical, geospatial, and network analysis. While expertise in these areas will make some aspects of this report easier to understand, results are presented in a clear manner that should be understandable to the lay audience. This research set out to answer three key questions: (1) How can we differentiate ISIS supporters and opponents on Twitter? (2) Who are they, and what are they saying? and (3) How are they connected, and who is important? Drawing conclusions from these results, we determine several recommendations that should be of interest to policymakers attempting to design counter-ISIS strategy in the social media space and beyond.

Funding for this study was provided, in part, by donors and by the independent research and development provisions of RAND's contracts for the operation of its U.S. Department of Defense federally funded research and development centers.

The research was conducted within the RAND National Security Research Division (NSRD) of the RAND Corporation. NSRD conducts research and analysis on defense and national security topics for the U.S. and allied defense, foreign policy, homeland security, and intelligence communities, and foundations and other nongovernmental organizations that support defense and national security analysis.

For more information on the RAND National Security Research Division, see www.rand.org/nsrd/ or contact the director (contact information is provided on the web page).

Contents

Figures

Tables

Summary

The Islamic State in Iraq and Syria (ISIS), like no other terrorist organization before, has used Twitter and other social media channels to broadcast its message, inspire followers, and recruit new fighters. Though much less heralded, ISIS opponents have also taken to Twitter to castigate the ISIS message. This report draws on publicly available Twitter data to examine this ongoing debate about ISIS on Arabic Twitter and to better understand the networks of ISIS supporters and opponents on Twitter.

To support the countermessaging effort and to more deeply understand ISIS supporters and opponents, this study uses a mixed-methods analytic approach to identify and characterize in detail both ISIS support and opposition networks on Twitter. This analytic approach draws on community detection algorithms that help detect interactive communities of Twitter users, lexical analysis that can identify key themes and content for large data sets, and social network analysis. This research set out to answer three key questions:

- How can we differentiate ISIS supporters and opponents on Twitter?
- Who are they, and what are they saying?
- How are they connected, and who is important?

How Can We Differentiate ISIS Supporters and Opponents on Twitter?

While ISIS has formally requested that its followers refer to it as *The Islamic State*, or الدولة الإسلامية, group detractors often use the abbreviation داعش, or *Daesh*. We examined whether these two terms would serve as putative measures of ISIS support or opposition, respectively. Using a ten-month sample of Twitter data, we lexically analyzed the content and key themes of users who mostly employ *Daesh* versus those who mostly use *Islamic State* in their tweets. As predicted, we found that frequent users of *Daesh* had content that was highly critical of ISIS, with users using such terms as *Terrorist Daesh, Kharijites, militants of Daesh, dogs of fire*, and *dogs of Baghdadi*. Users of *Islamic State*, however, used glowing terms such as *monotheists Mujahideen, Soldiers of the Caliphate*, and *lions of the Islamic State*. Other references to people, states, organizations, and location names were similarly predictive of support.

Drawing on this measure of support and opposition, we found that over the ten-month period (July 1, 2014, to April 30, 2015), ISIS opponents generally outnumber supporters six to one. On a daily basis, ISIS opponents outnumber supporters nearly ten to one. However, ISIS supporters routinely outtweet opponents, as they produce 50 percent more tweets per day. In examining the timeline of ISIS-related tweets, we found that the burning of the Jordanian pilot, Moath al-Kasabeh, sparked a huge upsurge in anti-ISIS tweets. In addition, at the end of our reporting period (March to April 2015), we found a significant reduction in the number of tweeting ISIS supporters and an upsurge in tweeting opponents.

Who Are They, and What Are They Saying?

We used lexical and network analysis in an iterative approach to identify and characterize different communities within the Twitter ISIS conversation. Drawing on community detection algorithms, we distilled 23 million tweets from 771,321 users into 36 distinct communities and ultimately into four major *metacommunities*. We then used lexical analysis to characterize the identities and prominent themes of these metacommunities.

Lexical analysis shows that these four metacommunities appear to belong to Shia, Syrian mujahideen, ISIS supporters, and Sunni.

- The Shia group condemns ISIS using historical Islamic terms and links to Saudi Arabia, expresses positive attitude toward the international coalition and Christians, and focuses on sectarianism and frustrations with Sunni/Shia divisions.
- Syrian Mujahideen supporters represent individuals throughout the Middle East who support the anti-Assad Syrian Mujahideen movement. These individuals have mixed attitudes toward the Islamic State and generally negative attitudes toward the international coalition for "supporting" the Syrian regime.
- The ISIS supporters frequently invoke threats against Islam, highlight positive themes that include religion, belonging, and positive terms, and use a variety of insults and derogatory terms to refer to Shia, the Syrian regime, the international community, and others. The analysis also suggests that ISIS supporters more actively adhere to good social media strategy by actively encouraging fellow supporters to "spread," "disseminate," and "link" messages to expand their reach and impact.
- The Sunni community is highly fractured in comparison with other metacommunities, and resonant themes are very different within the various Sunni subcommunities and appear to align with different Middle East nation-states. For example, one Sunni subcommunity appears to focus on themes of Egyptian nationalism, to include the threat of ISIS toward Egypt and concerns about the Muslim Brotherhood. Another group appears focused on Jordanian issues, with common themes including the ISIS threat to Egypt, the execution of the Jordanian pilot, Moath al-Kasabeh, and Jordan's role in the international coalition.

How Are They Connected, and Who Is Important?

We next applied social network analysis at the community level to assess relative strength and weaknesses of different connections between communities and how they were positioned with respect to one another. We found

- the core of the Syrian Mujahideen metacommunity serves as an important connection between the Shia metacommunity, some Sunni communities, and the ISIS Supporter metacommunity, who are otherwise disconnected. It is thus possible that individuals within the Syrian mujahideen community could serve as influencers of ISIS supporters and connect ISIS opponents together.

- The Egyptian, Saudi Arabian, and Gulf Cooperation Council (GCC) communities form the core of the Sunni metacommunity, which is by far more fractured than the Shia, Syrian Mujahideen, and ISIS Supporter metacommunities. In general, each subcommunity is concerned with its own specific issues, which could complicate constructing a coherent Sunni anti-ISIS countermessaging strategy.

- Within the Sunni subcommunities, the Yemeni community has the highest percentage of ISIS supporters and is sharply divided between ISIS supporters and opponents.

Implications and Recommendations

Based on these findings, we offer several recommendations for policymakers:

- Research institutions should continue to use the model of *Daesh* versus *Islamic State* for ISIS to gauge worldwide activity of ISIS supporters and opponents. The U.S. government may use such models to test the impact of anti-ISIS programs.

- ISIS opponents are plentiful but may require assistance from the U.S. State Department, in the form of social media trainings and other engagements, to enhance the effectiveness and reach of their messaging.[1] Of course, with al-Qa'ida and its affiliates counted among the ISIS opponents, care will have to be taken in selecting those suitable to train and empower.

- Twitter should continue its campaign of account suspensions: This campaign likely harasses ISIS Twitter users, forces them to lose valuable time reacquiring followers, and may ultimately push some to use social media channels that are far less public and accessible than Twitter.

- U.S. military Information Support Operations planners, as well as State Department messengers, should continue to highlight ISIS atrocities. The Twitter impact of the burning of the Jordanian pilot as well as previous findings suggesting a relation between ISIS atrocities and ISIS opposition on Twitter indicate that such atrocities may galvanize opponents. Note, however, ISIS clearly uses ultraviolence as a key component of its brand, and a messaging strategy, consequently, highlighting such actions risks playing into its hands (Winter, 2015). A more systematic examination of the causes behind these spikes and troughs, such as ISIS atrocities, would be valuable.

- Nations and organizations (such as U.S. military and State Department messengers) looking to countermessage ISIS on Twitter should tailor messages for and target them to specific communities: The ISIS Twitter universe is highly fragmented and consists of different communities that care about different topics. Countermessaging should take this into account with tailored communications to different communities.

---

[1] The U.S. and the international community already provide training in social media to select civil society members in the Muslim world, and such programs could be expanded and strengthened to provide a more robust effort to expand the voice of ISIS opponents.

Acknowledgments

Many individuals contributed to the completion of this report. We are particularly grateful to Eric K. Jones and Nicholas Pioch of ST Research for their informed advice and collaboration. We are also grateful for the assistance of Dr. Rand Waltzman, who recently managed Defense Advanced Research Projects Agency's Social Media in Strategic Communication program. We thank our reviewers, Angela O'Mahony, Sarah Meadows, and Daniel L. Byman. Finally, we are, of course, grateful to the RAND Corporation, which funded this study via internal research funding. Any errors are the sole responsibility of the study authors.

Abbreviations

Daesh	Arabic acronym for ISIS
GCC	Gulf Cooperation Council
IS	The Islamic State
ISIL	The Islamic State in Iraq and the Levant
ISIS	The Islamic State in Iraq and Syria (or al-Sham)
MC	metacommunity

CHAPTER ONE

Introduction

The Islamic State in Iraq and Syria (ISIS)[1] has made headlines with its dramatic and effective exploitation of social media. The organization has drawn on a variety of social networking applications to promote its cause, including Facebook, Instagram, Tumbler, Ask.fm, and, most prominently, Twitter. It has used Twitter to disseminate slick yet violence-ridden propaganda videos, promote its religious ideology and state-building efforts, and make one-on-one connections with prospective recruits. As of late 2014, the group drew on at least 46,000 individual Twitter accounts worldwide and capitalized on a small group of "hyperactive users" whose high volume and concentrated bursts of Tweets help land ISIS hashtags and messages on top trending charts (Berger and Morgan, 2015). It has also benefited from small cells of influencers or "disseminators" who, though outside the ISIS area of operations, play an outsize role in providing "encouragement, justification, and religious legitimacy for fighting" (Carter, Maher, and Neumann, 2014).

Its social media prowess has quite possibly played a part in ISIS's enormous success in recruitment.[2] Over 30,000 foreign fighters, 4,500 of whom are Westerners, have flocked to the ISIS cause (Norton-Taylor, 2015). Approximately 250 Americans have left the United States to join ISIS, and others have heeded ISIS calls for violence (Paquette, 2015). ISIS operatives have launched a variety of deadly attacks, most notably the Brussels airport and subway bombings of March 22, 2016, which killed 32 individuals, and the Paris attacks of November 13, 2015, which resulted in 130 fatalities. There was also the attack in San Bernardino, California, on December 2, 2015, which killed 14. Other attacks in the United States include that at the Mohammad cartoon rally in Garland, Texas, an attempted knife assault against law enforcement in Boston, and a hatchet assault against police officers in New York City. ISIS-inspired attacks have also occurred in many other places, including Canada, Australia, Tunisia, Turkey, and Egypt (Yourish, Watkins, and Giratikanon, 2016).

While Twitter serves ISIS propaganda and aids its goals, the availability of tweets to the broader public also opens a unique window into the social networks of extremist supporters and gives researchers the ability to study the impact of extremist messaging. In addition to exposing ISIS supporters, Twitter provides an opportunity to assess the structure and messaging of ISIS opponents, since it is home not only to ISIS recruiters and advocates but also to

---

[1]   Also known as the Islamic State (IS), the Islamic State in Iraq and the Levant (ISIL), and by its Arabic acronym, *Daesh*. We choose to use the term *ISIS* to maintain internal consistency within this report, but note that the term used to refer to ISIS is quite important, as shown in our later analysis.

[2]   Few, if any, empirical examinations provide a concrete depiction of what radicalization to the ISIS cause entails and the degree to which this radicalization is prompted by online versus offline networks. For this reason, we caveat the potential role of social media in ISIS recruitment.

many in the Middle East who do not support the Islamic State.[3] While ISIS supporters talk up themes of defending Islam, recruiting new fighters, promoting state-building efforts, and critiquing the West, ISIS opponents fight back by accusing ISIS of subverting Islam, highlighting ISIS violence, and trumpeting its terrorist threat.

Part of countering ISIS in the real world is countering its messaging online. However, it is well recognized that overt U.S. messaging against ISIS, even if it uses the same themes highlighted above, will likely fall flat. Not only does the United States have poor overall credibility in the region, but it is also poorly positioned to directly address theological or other various factors that motivate young recruits (Helmus, York, and Chalk, 2013; Miller, 2015). Because of this, it is critical for the United States and its international partners to work with influential communities in the region that can more effectively and credibly counter the ISIS narrative. A successful counter-ISIS messaging campaign requires understanding of the unique audience segments that constitute both the ISIS supporter and ISIS opposition networks, as well as the key themes that motivate them.

To support the countermessaging effort and the general effort to more deeply understand ISIS supporters and opponents, this study uses a mixed-methods analytic approach to identify and characterize in detail both ISIS support and ISIS opposition networks on Twitter.

Approach

This study focused on Arabic-language tweets and Twitter networks. We queried a historical Twitter database for Arabic-language tweets that referenced ISIS during the time period of July 1, 2014, to April 30, 2015 (approximately from al-Baghdadi's declaration of the Caliphate to the end of April the next year), retrieving over 23 million tweets.[4] Our search terms included 35 common grammatical variations on the terms الدولة الإسلامية (*Islamic State*) and داعش (*Daesh*). Since our search terms were all in Arabic, most of the tweets were also in Arabic, although a few were in English or other languages with the Arabic terms.[5] The data returned include the content of the tweet itself, the username and account number of the user who posted it, any public profile information the user may have had at the time, and associated metadata like time, location, platform used, etc. Note that these data include retweets as well as original tweets.

Using these data, we attempted to answer three key questions: (1) How can we differentiate ISIS supporters and opponents on Twitter? (2) Who are they, and what are they saying?

---

[3]   An October 2014 in-person survey of residents in Egypt, Saudi Arabia, and Lebanon suggested that only 3 percent of respondents support ISIS (Pollock, 2015). Likewise, a November 2014 telephone survey of residents in Tunisia, Egypt, Palestine, Jordan, Saudi Arabia, Lebanon, and Iraq suggested that approximately 11 percent express positive attitudes toward ISIS with 85 percent expressing negative attitudes (Arab Opinion Project, 2014).

[4]   See Appendix A for the entire list of search terms and code used to query the Twitter database.

[5]   It should be recognized that only a minority of the Arab populations use Twitter. According to the *Arab Social Media Report* published in 2014, there are 5,797,500 Twitter users in the Arab world. Approximately 7.6 percent of Kuwaitis (225,000), 6.5 percent of Saudis (1.9 million), 4.9 percent of United Arab Emirates citizens (401,000), 1.35 percent of Jordanians (88,800), and 0.6 percent of Egyptians (519,000) actively use Twitter. Approximately 36.6 percent of Twitter users are female ("Twitter in the Arab Region," undated). Consequently, while these findings are certainly pertinent to ISIS Twitter networks, they should not be construed as representative of the general Arab population.

(3) How are they connected, and who is important? We specify our general approach to answering each of these questions next (see appendixes for greater methodological detail).

How Can We Differentiate ISIS Supporters and Opponents on Twitter?

Anecdotal evidence suggests that the usage of the full Arabic name for the Islamic State, الدولة الإسلامية, serves as an indicator of ISIS support, while use of the abbreviation, داعش, serves as an indicator of ISIS opposition. We quantitatively validate this hypothesis by applying automated lexical analysis to our sample of Twitter data, determining both the relative number of supporters and opponents of ISIS on Twitter and measuring their prolificacy.[6] Specifically, we isolated one sample of data comprising individuals who refer to *Islamic State* in 80 percent of their tweets and others who refer to *Daesh* in 80 percent of their tweets. In order to validate that the use of these terms indicates ISIS support and opposition, respectively, we then used lexical analysis methods such as log likelihood scores and collocates (commonly co-occurring word pairs) to test the content of these two samples against each other. Finally, having confirmed this hypothesis, we compared the two samples in terms of relative size, total tweet count, and active Twitter users per day. We find that ISIS opponents outnumber supporters six to one, but ISIS supporters are more active, generating 50 percent more tweets per day.

Who Are They, and What Are They Saying?

Applying lexical and network analysis in an iterative approach to our large Twitter data set, we find and characterize different communities within the Twitter ISIS conversation. To do this, we created a mentions network—a directed, weighted network in which each node represents a user and each edge the number of mentions between users. We then used an iterative series of Clauset-Newman-Moore community detection algorithms to winnow down the data set from a mentions network of 771,321 users and 3,336,589 mentions to the four most salient communities of closely connected Twitter users. We then applied lexical analysis to each of these communities to understand common Twitter themes and broadly identify the group of users.

We found that the top four communities (referred to as *metacommunities*) we identified appeared to belong to the Shia, Syrian mujahideen, ISIS supporters, and Sunni. While the three other communities are fairly cohesive, the Sunni community is highly fractured, and resonant themes are very different within the various Sunni subcommunities. These subcommunities, in general, appear organized along nationalistic lines with individual subcommunities representing Yemen, Libya, Saudi Arabia, Jordan, Egypt, and Tunisia. To design an effective countermessaging strategy, it is important to know which themes are significant within each community, and the extent to which each community supports or opposes ISIS; our analysis uses a highly efficient, blended human and automated approach to answer these questions.

How Are They Connected, and Who Is Important?

Finally, we apply techniques from social network analysis to determine the relative strength and weaknesses of connections between specific communities and highlight the different roles that each community plays within the Twitter conversation. To do this, we examine the community network, where each node in the network represents an entire community of user accounts, and the edges between communities aggregate the mentions between users in those

---

[6]   This hypothesis was also validated by Magdy, Darwish, and Weber (2015) with a smaller sample and a more manual approach.

respective communities. We specifically focus on the interrelationship of the Shia, ISIS Supporter, and Syrian Mujahideen metacommunities and the individual Sunni communities. Our analysis also further explores the individual Sunni communities that make up the Sunni metacommunity by examining key message themes, percentage of participants who are ISIS supporters versus opponents, and the geospatial analysis of these communities.

One caveat of this study's analysis is that the study's focus on Arabic-language Twitter obviously fails to address the broader English and even multilingual ISIS conversation. As of 2013, 62.1 percent of tweets in the Arab region were in Arabic, in comparison with 32.6 percent in English ("Transforming Education in the Arab World," 2013). This percentage of English-language tweets will likely be even higher among Arab populations residing in Europe and the United States. Consequently, it will obviously be necessary to replicate this study's findings with an English-language sample.

That said, a major headline of this analysis is that the Syrian mujahideen community appears to be particularly important to this core network, due to its position between ISIS supporters and potentially more-moderate Sunni communities. It is possible that it could serve as an important influencer node to sway ISIS supporters with countermessaging.

These insights are important in determining how to target ISIS supporters, reinforce ISIS opponents, and sway the broad middle ground. Applying the same techniques at a more granular level, we also identify key users who are highly influential within specific communities. As with our lexical analysis, this approach blends automated and human analysis to quickly gain useful insights from a very large data set.

Outline of This Report

We attempt to answer these three questions in chronological order. Chapter Two presents the analysis on "How can we differentiate ISIS supporters and opponents on Twitter?" Chapter Three presents the analysis on "Who are they and what are they saying?" Chapter Four presents findings from our examination of "How are they connected and who is important?" In Chapter Five, we present implications of these findings and offer a set of recommendations for decisionmakers. In addition, given the technical nature of this report, we use appendixes to provide greater detail on methods and findings. Appendix A provides a detailed description of the search parameters used to acquire the Twitter data sample used in this report. Appendix B provides a thorough description of our analytic methods used in the lexical and social network analysis. Finally, we use Appendix C to present detailed analysis of the individual Sunni communities (Jordan, Egypt, Tunisia, Libya, etc.) that make up the larger Sunni metacommunity.

CHAPTER TWO

ISIS Supporters and Opponents on Twitter

On June 29, 2014, ISIS declared itself a caliphate and changed its name from *Islamic State in Iraq and the Levant* to *The Islamic State* (الدولة الإسلامية), decreeing: "Accordingly, the 'Iraq and Shām [Levant]' in the name of the Islamic State is henceforth removed from all official deliberations and communications, and the official name is the Islamic State from the date of this declaration" ("This Is the Promise of Allah," 2014). ISIS fighters and media outlets were quick to use the new name. Others in the Middle East, however, used *Daesh* (داعش) to refer to ISIS, forming an acronym from the letters of the name in Arabic, "al-Dawla al-Islamiya fi Iraq wa al-Sham." Formal Arabic language makes little use of acronyms, and the application of an acronym in references to the Islamic State carried pejorative connotations. Indeed, ISIS formally objected to its usage ("Isis, Isil or Da'ish? What to Call Militants in Iraq," 2014).

Using lexical analysis, we validated the anecdotal evidence that ISIS supporters overwhelmingly use the term *The Islamic State* (الدولة الإسلامية) while opponents tend to use the acronym *Daesh* (داعش) and created a quick test to categorize individual Twitter accounts as pro- or anti-ISIS based on their terminology history.[1] With this categorization, we present a rough map of the supporters and opponents to ISIS on Twitter according to their language, activity, and geographic location.

Using Terminology to Find ISIS Supporters and Opponents

Pulling from the Twitter fire hose tweets that referenced *The Islamic State* (الدولة الإسلامية) or *Daesh* (داعش) from July 1, 2014, through April 30, 2015, we created a data set of over 23 million tweets and associated metadata, from over 771,000 distinct user accounts.[2] For more detail on our data collection methodology, see Appendix A.

From this data set, we created two bodies of text to validate the Islamic State versus Daesh hypothesis. The first was composed of all tweets from users who employed *Islamic State* or a

---

[1] Magdy, Darwish, and Weber (2015) found that it is possible to differentiate between ISIS supporters and opponents by the way their tweets refer to the organization. This study identified a set of Twitter users who (1) authored ten or more tweets that mentioned ISIS, and (2) strictly used either the long name (*Islamic State*) or the abbreviated name of ISIS in at least 70 percent of their tweets that mentioned the group. Using this data set, they determined that of those tweets that referenced the abbreviated name, 77.3 percent were anti-ISIS, 7.5 percent were pro-ISIS, and 15.2 percent were neutral/spam. Of those tweets that primarily referenced the *Islamic State*, 1.2 percent were anti-ISIS, 93.1 percent were pro-ISIS, and 5.7 percent were neutral/spam. While these results are similar to ours, our study used a much larger data set and an automated approach.

[2] Note that these are distinct user accounts, not users. It has become common practice for ISIS supporters to create multiple Twitter accounts as backup as they are suspended from Twitter.

related term to refer to ISIS in at least 80 percent of their tweets (4 million tweets with 67 million words), and the other was composed of all tweets from users who employed *Daesh* or a related term to refer to the organization in at least 80 percent of their tweets (18 million tweets with 316 million words). Applying lexical analysis methods such as log likelihood scores and collocates[3] to test these two corpora against each other, we determined that, in Arabic, the use of *Islamic State* is an indicator for support for ISIS, while *Daesh* is an indicator for opposition to the organization. The *Islamic State* users used glowing terms to refer to members of the organization; echoed phrases from ISIS propaganda, including its motto and guiding principle; and tweeted hashtags supporting the organization. In contrast, the *Daesh* users described ISIS members in derogatory terms; spoke about fighting the organization; and tweeted hashtags that accused ISIS of atrocities and collusion with undesirable actors. Table 2.1 presents the differing language used by the two groups of Twitter users when talking about ISIS.

The corpora continued the support-opposition divide with respect to which people and organizations they disproportionately mentioned. The *Islamic State* users referenced top leadership of ISIS other than Abu Bakr al-Baghdadi, as well as Jabhat al-Nusra and an ISIS media outlet. They also mentioned the usernames of Twitter accounts that supported ISIS and had been suspended. While the *Daesh* users referenced ISIS "caliph" Abu Bakr al-Baghdadi, they also referenced Sunni Saudi establishment clerics, Saudi and United Arab Emirates news out-

Table 2.1
Differing References to ISIS

Content	Users of *Islamic State*	Users of *Daesh*
ISIS members	monotheists [*muwahideen*, believers in the oneness of God] mujahideen soldiers of the caliphate lions of the Islamic State martyrdom-seeker [*istishaadi*, positive term for a suicide bomber]	the terrorist Daesh the Kharijites of Daesh, today's Kharijites, Kharijites [derogatory term for Sunni extremists] the militants of Daesh dogs of fire dogs of Baghdadi
ISIS phrases	in the shadow of the caliphate [phrase used in ISIS propaganda] O Supporters, supporters of the Islamic State, the brotherhood of supporters in all corners of the world may God accept him [said about martyrs] prophetic methodology, in accordance with the prophetic methodology [ISIS "guiding principle"] Baqiya [Remaining, first half of the ISIS motto]	crimes of Daesh to fight Daesh to confront Daesh strike Daesh
Hashtags about ISIS	#Remaining_and_expanding [*Baqiya wa Tatamudud*, the ISIS motto] #The_global_campaign_to_support_the_Islamic_State #The_media_front_to_support_the_Islamic_State	#Terrorist_Daesh_Organization #Daesh_does_not_attack_Iran #Daesh_is_a_Russian_and_Iranian_creation #Daesh_assaults_a_female_tourist #Daesh_and_Iran_are_against_Saudi_Arabia #arrest_of_a_Daesh_cell_in_Tamir [Saudi city] #Daesh_burns_the_Jordanian_pilot #Daesh_enslaves_the_Muslims_of_Deir_al-Zour

SOURCE: RAND analysis, Twitter data from July 2014 to May 2015.

---

[3]   See Appendix B for a detailed discussion of the lexical analysis methods employed.

lets, the Jordanian pilot burned alive by ISIS, and a range of armed actors in the Syrian conflict opposed to ISIS, as shown in Table 2.2.

The distinctive language the two groups used to refer to ISIS's adversaries also showed a clear divide along pro-ISIS and anti-ISIS lines. The *Islamic State* users' references to the Syrian regime, the Iraqi government, Arab states, and Western actors were derogatory and employed textbook phrases from ISIS propaganda. The *Daesh* users' mentions of these actors instead emphasized secular institutions and governance structures, using more neutral or even positive language, as shown in Table 2.3.

However, a few outliers contradicted the trend of *Islamic State* indicating support and *Daesh* indicating opposition. The hashtag #Al-Baghdadi_son_of_a_whore, a derogatory reference to ISIS caliph Abu Bakr al-Baghdadi, was conspicuously overpresent in the *Islamic State* corpus. In turn, the hashtag #Pray_for_the_Daesh_Organization was conspicuously overpresent in the *Daesh* corpus. This last hashtag was particularly ambiguous; it may have originally been a message of support for ISIS, or it may have urged users to pray for ISIS to turn from its

Table 2.2
Differing References to People, Users, and Organizations

Content	Users of *Islamic State*	Users of *Daesh*
People	Muhamad al-Adnani, ISIS spokesperson Muhamad al-Golani, Jabhat al-Nusra leader	Abu Bakr al-Baghdadi, ISIS "caliph" Mohamad_al-Arefe, Sunni Saudi cleric Saudi al-Shuraim and Abdul Rahman al-Sudias, establishment Sunni Saudi imams #Fayes_al-Maliki, Saudi actor, public ambassador to the Gulf "the Jordanian pilot," Moath al-Kasabeh [Jordanian pilot burned alive by ISIS] Bashar al-Assad
Users	@aamaq_twitt, suspended user presumably affiliated with A'maq News @asawirtimedia, suspended ISIS media outlet @khilafapress, suspended pro-ISIS account	@saleelalmajd1, self-described "Shami [Syrian] voice from the jihadi current who tweets from behind the scenes" @alamawi, supports Free Syrian Army (FSA), listed location of Syria @mbc8pm, Saudi-based channel @groouprt, suspended user, but name suggests a service for buying retweets
Non-ISIS groups	Jabhat al-Nusra	Muslim Brotherhood, Sunni transnational organization with roots in Egypt Ansar Beit al-Muqadis [ABM, Egyptian terror group that after joining ISIS officially became "Sinai Province"] Jabhat al-Nusra the Free Army [FSA, Free Syrian Army] the Syrian Observer Hizbullah
Media outlets	#A'maq_Agency, pro-ISIS media outlet	#Routana_Khalijia, Routana, United Arab Emirates–based television channel

SOURCE: RAND analysis, Twitter data from July 2014 to May 2015.

Table 2.3
Differing References to ISIS's Adversaries

Adversary	Users of *Islamic State*	Users of *Daesh*
Syria	*Rafidha, Rawafidh* [derogatory term for Shia, used by ISIS] *Nusayri*, the Nusayri regime [derogatory term for Alawi, used by ISIS to describe the Assad regime]	the Syrian army, the Syrian regime, the Syrian people, the rebels [the more secular way of referring to the Syrian opposition, instead of mujahideen]
Iraq	*Safavid*, the Safavid army [derogatory term for Iranian, used by ISIS to describe Iran and those Iran supports]	the Iraqi army, *al-Hashd al-Sha'bi* [PMF, the Popular Mobilization Forces]
Arab states	apostate, the apostates [used by ISIS to describe Sunnis who oppose ISIS], the tyrants [*tawaghit*, term used by ISIS to describe Arab rulers]	the Arab nations, Defense Minister, Foreign Minister, Air Defense
The West	Crusader, the Crusader coalition [Crusader being a derogatory term for Christian, used by ISIS to describe the West]	the international coalition, Security Council, airstrike

SOURCE: RAND analysis, Twitter data from July 2014 to May 2015.

errant ways. Further analysis found that the majority of the tweets in which this hashtag was used were spam.[4]

Despite the outliers, it is clear from the lexical analysis above that the terminology in a given Twitter user's tweet history can serve as a quick indicator for support or opposition to ISIS. Furthermore, supporters and opponents to ISIS use clearly distinct language to refer to people, organizations, and ISIS's adversaries, indicating the need to create different types of messages using distinct language in targeting the two groups, at least for countermessaging efforts in Arabic.

ISIS Supporters and Opponents: Activity and Location

With the ability to quickly characterize individual users (and tweets) based on the terminology employed to refer to ISIS, we were able to divide our entire data set (23 million tweets, more than 770,000 users) into two groups: ISIS supporters and ISIS opponents.[5] We found approximately 18.8 million tweets to be anti-ISIS, and approximately 4.5 million pro-ISIS tweets. Within these, we characterized 471,492 user accounts as anti-ISIS and 75,946 user accounts as pro-ISIS, approximately a 6:1 ratio of opponents to supporters. Note that the actual ratio may in fact be larger, as ISIS supporters tend to operate multiple Twitter accounts, establishing new ones as old ones are suspended.

Our numbers are roughly consistent with two previous studies, one of which drew on a specially curated set of Twitter accounts, finding a ratio of 4:1 for users (Magdy, Darwish, and Weber, 2015), and another that discovered a 4:1 opposition-to-support ratio for tweets (Voices from the Blogs, 2014).

---

[4] The practice of co-opting popular hashtags for the purposes of selling goods or services is quite common on Twitter. This is likely an example of such activity.

[5] Note that there are some tweets and users that employ both terms. However, these numbers were quite small compared with the pro- and anti-ISIS groups.

Despite the larger number of opponents, ISIS supporters still seem to overwhelm Twitter with their content. This is based in part on their Twitter activity: tweeting, on average, 60 times per day, while opponents tweet 40 times per day—and using a sophisticated social media–savvy strategy (as discussed in the next chapter). Figures 2.1 and 2.2 show the daily number of active Twitter accounts for both groups; note the order of magnitude difference in active daily users. Figure 2.1 ranges from 0 to 89,129 tweets per day, while Figure 2.2 ranges from 0 to 2,958 tweets per day.

There is a large spike in ISIS opponents in February 2015, which corresponds to the release of the video depicting the burning of the Jordanian pilot Moath al-Kasabeh. We see a corresponding gradual decrease in the number of active ISIS supporters beginning shortly thereafter. However, it is unclear without further analysis whether this is due to ISIS atrocities like the pilot burning or the Twitter account suspension campaign, which began in March 2015.

It is also possible to characterize the ISIS support and opposition Twitter users based on their geographic location, at least for those tweets that are geotagged. Using these metadata, we show in the two maps in Figure 2.3 the global dispersion of tweets from users that we characterize as pro- or anti-ISIS. Each dot corresponds to an individual tweet, with the color intensity indicating the percentage of that user's tweet history that is either *Islamic State* or *Daesh*.

Figure 2.1
Active Twitter Users (ISIS Opponents), per Day

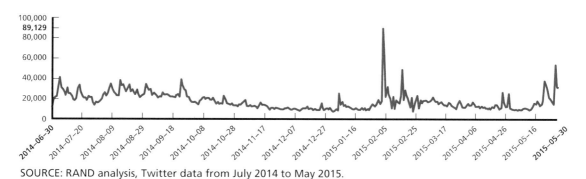

SOURCE: RAND analysis, Twitter data from July 2014 to May 2015.
RAND *RR1328-2.1*

Figure 2.2
Active Twitter Users (ISIS Supporters), per Day

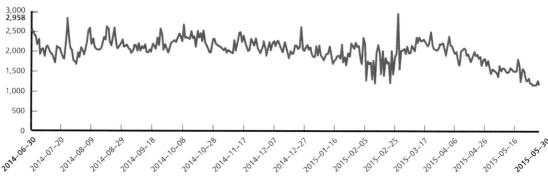

SOURCE: RAND analysis, Twitter data from July 2014 to May 2015.
RAND *RR1328-2.2*

Figure 2.3
Geospatial Analysis of Twitter Supporters and Opponents

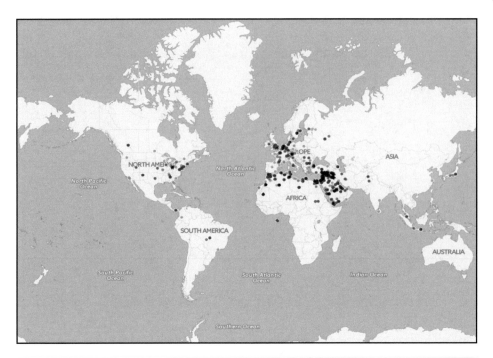

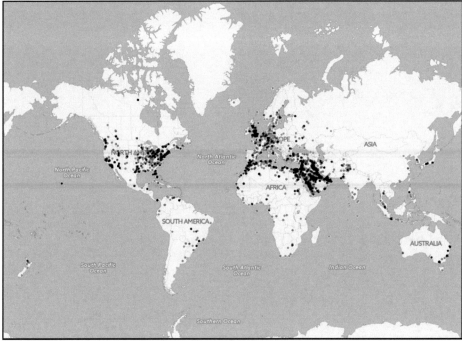

SOURCE: RAND analysis, Twitter data from July 2014 to May 2015.
NOTE: ISIS supporters are shown in shades of red in the first map, while ISIS opponents are
shown in green in the second. Color intensity reflects the corresponding user's percentage of
Islamic State or *Daesh* tweets, respectively.
RAND *RR1328-2.3*

While the percentage of geotagged tweets is low (under 1 percent of our total data set), we can still use these metadata to determine the relative global spread of supporters versus opponents. From the maps in the figure, it appears that ISIS opponents are far more globally diverse, while ISIS supporters tend to be concentrated in the Middle East. However, this single observation should not be used to justify particular actions, since prior research suggests that geotagged tweets may not be representative of broader population estimates (Momin et al., 2015). Rather, this apparent pattern indicates the need for further research on the global reach of ISIS supporters and opponents, using more sophisticated techniques such as geoinference.

Summary

In summary, we found that the use of the Arabic terms for *The Islamic State* and *Daesh* within individual tweets appears to differentiate ISIS supporters and opponents, respectively. Between July 1, 2014, and April 30, 2015, the total number of ISIS opponents outnumbered supporters six to one. However, this ratio increases to nearly ten to one when one considers the number of active Twitter users per day. Though outnumbered, ISIS supporters routinely outtweet opponents, as they produce 50 percent more tweets per day. In addition, it was noteworthy that the burning of the Jordanian pilot Moath al-Kasabeh sparked a huge upsurge in anti-ISIS tweets. Further, at the end of our reporting period, we found a significant reduction in the number of tweeting ISIS supporters and an upsurge in tweeting opponents.

CHAPTER THREE

ISIS Debate: Community Content

Knowing the relative number of ISIS opponents and supporters on Twitter is valuable, but to design an appropriate countermessaging strategy to ISIS, it is more important to be able to characterize those opponents and supporters—to know what sorts of messages will resonate with them, their background, and what topics are likely to elicit interest versus those that will only provoke anger. To do this deeper sort of analysis on our data set, we combined network and lexical analysis methods, first determining the structure of the conversation about ISIS on Twitter and then characterizing the communities found within that structure according to their lexical distinctions.

To focus on the conversation between users on Twitter, we created a *mentions* network—a directed, weighted network in which each node represents a user and each edge the number of mentions between users.[1] Using this approach, we generated a network of 771,321 nodes and 3,336,589 weighted edges from our original data set of approximately 23 million tweets. Note that there are far fewer edges than tweets; some edges include more than one mention, and many tweets do not include any mentions at all and thus are not included in the data set.

We determined that there were 21,442 *communities* within the mentions network, using the Clauset-Newman-Moore community detection algorithm (see Appendix B for details on this and other algorithms used in the study). Each of these communities represents a group of Twitter user accounts that are more tightly connected to each other—meaning they are mentioning each other more often—than they are to the others in the network. Some of these communities were quite large, with roughly 127,000 members, while many were very small, with only one or two members.

In order to characterize these communities, we repeated the community detection algorithm, this time on the network of communities,[2] resulting in four *metacommunities* (see Figure 3.1). The composition of each of these metacommunities is shown in Table 3.1. Using lexical analysis, we characterized each metacommunity according to the distinctive language used in that community's tweets (see Appendix B for more detail on the specific methods used), labeling the four communities Shia, Syrian Mujahideen, ISIS Supporters, and Sunni States based on our results, as shown in Figure 3.2.

---

[1]   In a Twitter mention, a user will include in the tweet content *@username*, the user that the original poster wants to mention. This is also used in the standard format of retweets, attributing content to the original author. Thus, the mentions network contains both general mentions and retweets.

[2]   This is a common network analysis technique used for very large data sets, usually referred to as a "community of communities" analysis. In the community network, each node represents a community (potentially thousands of user accounts) and each directed, weighted edge the mentions between members of respective communities.

As with the ISIS supporter and opponent analysis in the previous chapter, we plotted the Twitter activity for all four metacommunities (as shown in Figure 3.3). We see that the two most strongly anti-ISIS groups, Shia and Sunni States, have almost identical activity patterns, potentially indicating that the same events caught both groups' attention. Clearly visible on this plot and common to all four metacommunities is the sudden surge in the number of active users on February 3, 2015, reflecting the release of the video of Moath al-Kasabeh being burned alive. Until this point, the ISIS Supporters and Syrian Mujahideen activity had closely resembled each other. After mid-February, the ISIS Supporters activity decreased and the Syrian Mujahideen activity grew and more closely resembled the Shia and Sunni groups. However,

Figure 3.1
Tweets to Communities Methodology

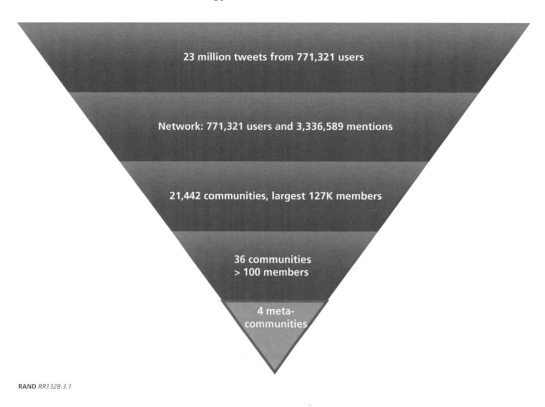

23 million tweets from 771,321 users

Network: 771,321 users and 3,336,589 mentions

21,442 communities, largest 127K members

36 communities
> 100 members

4 meta-
communities

RAND *RR1328-3.1*

Table 3.1
Metacommunity Composition

Metacommunity Label	Users	Tweets	Words	Spam (%)
Shia	115,934	5,043,916	88,885,891	1
Syrian Mujahideen	79,480	3,980,629	72,639,564	4
ISIS Supporters	72,457	6,412,721	104,490,012	7
Sunni States	379,778	18,638,101	299,322,234	11
Total, metacommunities	647,649	34,075,367	565,337,701	8

SOURCE: RAND analysis, Twitter data from July 2014 to May 2015.

NOTE: Spam is defined as tweets from users who have more than 10,000 tweets in the sample.

Figure 3.2
Community of Communities (Metacommunities) Network

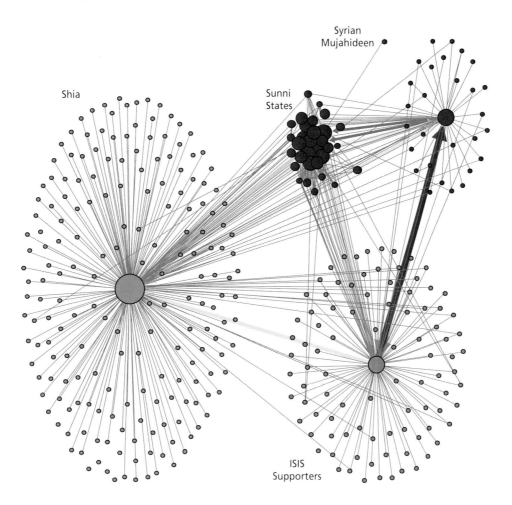

SOURCE: RAND analysis, Twitter data from July 2014 to May 2015.
NOTE: In this figure, each node represents a community, with the size of the node indicating the size of the community (i.e., the number of user accounts belonging to that community). Nodes are grouped and colored by metacommunity. Edge color indicates relative number of tweets between communities, with red indicating very large, orange large, yellow moderate, and gray small.
RAND *RR1328-3.2*

Figure 3.3
Metacommunity Active Users (per Day)

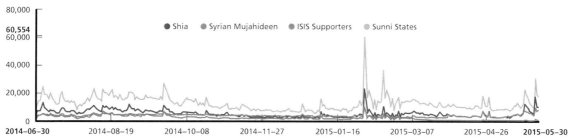

SOURCE: RAND analysis, Twitter data from July 2014 to May 2015.
RAND *RR1328-3.3*

it is not clear without further lexical analysis whether this decrease in active support was due to the increased publicity surrounding ISIS atrocities or to the Twitter suspension campaign.

Shia Distinct Messaging and Themes

Shown in teal in Figure 3.2, the Shia metacommunity's identity was clear from the lexical analysis. Colloquial terms and frequently mentioned location names suggested Iraqi, Lebanese, and Gulf nationalities. Users lionized militant organizations that are primarily Shia, supported by Iran, and generally criticized by Sunni, such as the Syrian Arab Army, Iraqi militas *'Asa'ib Ahl al-Haq* and *Kata'ib Hizbullah*, and Lebanese Hizbullah.[3] The polite term for Shia, which is *Shia*, was vastly overpresent in this community's talk.[4] Hassan Nasrallah, the leader of Hizbullah, appeared to be a key figure.[5] The metacommunity's attitude toward the international community and Christians was fairly positive, with polite references to the *international coalition*, and *Christians* (rather than *Crusaders*). Most of these mentions criticized ISIS attacks against Christians. References to Sunnis ranged from positive but reserved (e.g., "The truth is that Daesh is attacking and killing the Sunni people, while the Shia army is the one protecting them") to negative (e.g., "the Sunni people in Iraq betrayed their country").

The Shia metacommunity condemned ISIS by using Islamic-historical terms and by linking it with Saudi Arabia. It denigrated ISIS members as being *takfiiris*, a term that accuses them of declaring other Muslims to be apostates, and *Kharijites*, a splinter movement in the early Islamic period whose members rejected the authority of any ruler who deviated from their interpretation of Islam. Users equated ISIS and Jabhat al-Nusra, as well as ISIS and al-Qa'ida, condemning them as "two sides of the same coin." Anti-Saudiism, linked with anti-Sunnism, also resonated; users called ISIS members *Wahhabis*, the negative term for members of the Saudi branch of Sunnism.[6] This metacommunity also condemned ISIS members as terrorists, criminals, cowards, scum, and rats.

Syrian Mujahideen Distinct Messaging and Themes

The second metacommunity, named *Syrian Mujahideen*, is shown in purple in Figure 3.2. It was primarily composed of supporters of the Syrian mujahideen and those who are fighting against the Syrian regime, especially the Free Syrian Army, Jabhat al-Nusra, and Jaysh al-Islam. Elements within this metacommunity both support and oppose ISIS.

---

[3]   These Shia forces' fighters were called "heroes," and users also used the nickname for Lebanese Hizbullah popular with its supporters, "The Resistance." Users also supported the Electronic Iraqi Army and the Jerusalem Brigades (*Saraya al-Quds*), an armed Palestinian organization.

[4]   Likewise, negative Shia terms such as "*Safavid*," an Arab term for Iranian, and "*Rawafidh*," a pejorative Sunni reference for Shia, were conspicuously absent.

[5]   In addition, many Twitter usernames repeated over and over included Shia-based news organizations and other prominent Shia figures and organizations. Saddam Hussein was also mentioned frequently, usually as a neutral historical or locational reference point with a negative cast, as in the following tweet: "a newspaper discovered that all the leaders of Daesh are the officers of Saddam."

[6]   The hashtag #Launch_a_rumor_that_the_Saudis_believe was also popular.

Overpresent location names were almost all Syria-specific, such as Aleppo, Ayn al-Arab, al-Qalamoun, Ghouta, and #Camp_Yarmouk, a Palestinian camp in Damascus. Users lionized Syrian rebel groups, including the Free Syrian Army and the Islamic Front.[7] Twitter usernames repeated over and over again included a "writer and researcher" who tweets in support of the Syrian revolution and against Shia, a self-described "Shami voice from the jihadi current who tweets from behind the scenes," and the Twitter account of the "Syrian Revolution Forum." Most tweets that referenced the international coalition denounced it, claiming that it benefited the Assad regime.[8]

Users called fighters from rebel groups *mujahideen*, and *the revolutionaries*. They made positive appeals such as *honor* and *pride* and infused this positive messaging with religious and Islamic terms such as *God is Great* and *the hope of the coming **umma***, which means the Muslim community. References to the Syrian regime were negative, some including the reference *the **Nusayri** regime*, a derogatory term for the Alawi sect, which controls the Syrian regime.

Support for ISIS was mixed. Some tweets included respectful references like *soldiers of the Islamic State, the Islamic caliphate*, and *the caliphate and the hope of* the Muslim community. But this was counteracted by many overpresent anti-IS phrases calling ISIS members *Kharijites*, and *dogs of the people of fire*. One popular hashtag, #Bashar_of_Daesh_burns_Deir_al-Zour, discredits ISIS by linking it with the Syrian regime's atrocities. The term *terrorists* was conspicuously underpresent.

ISIS Supporters Distinct Messaging and Themes

The third metacommunity, *ISIS Supporters*, shown in green in Figure 3.2, was composed of virulent ISIS supporters. Overpresent location names included ISIS focus-points such as "Raqqa Province," Kobani, Ayn al-Arab, Baiji, Sinai, and Iraq. In addition to Abu Bakr al-Baghdadi, whose name came up in most metacommunities, official ISIS spokesperson Abu Muhammad al-Adnani and Jabhat al-Nusra leader Abu Muhammad al-Julani featured very prominently. Almost all overpresent usernames belonged to suspended accounts, including ISIS media outlets and prominent pro-IS accounts. Clearly pro-ISIS terms and phrases included *Remaining and Expanding* (*Baqiya wa Tatamadud*), the oath of allegiance to the caliph (*ba'ya*), *the prophetic methodology*, which ISIS claims is its guiding principle, *supporters of the Islamic State*, and #The_global_campaign_to_support_the_Islamic_State.

The ISIS supporters demonstrated a more self-aware social media strategy than any of the other groups, with disproportionately high usage of social media terms such as *spread*, *link, breaking news, media office, now released*, and *pictorial evidence* overrepresented, in addition to hashtags like #Support_the_accounts_of_the_supporters_of_the_Islamic_State and #support_the_supporters_in_vexing_the_infidels.

---

[7] Key figures included Zahran Alyoush, the leader of the Islamic Front and commander of Jaysh al-Islam, and Abu Muhammad al-Julani, the leader of Jabhat al-Nusra.

[8] One message, retweeted over 300 times, read: "The Islamic State takes the lead in Deir al-Zour, while the planes of the coalition bomb as if in support of Assad's forces, and protect the Deir al-Zour airport from falling," and another commonly retweeted tweet asked: "The coalition brought together 40 states in order to fight Daesh, yet this coalition was not formed in order to save the Muslims and their children from the massacres of Bashar al-Assad??"

Table 3.2
ISIS Language

Entity	ISIS Term
Syrian government	the *Nusayri* regime
International community	Crusaders, the Crusader-Arab coalition
Arab state rulers	the tyrants (*al-Tawaghit*)
Sunnis who do not support ISIS	apostates (*al-murtadin*)
Shia	*Rawafidh*; literally translated as *rejectionists*
Iran and Iraq	Persian, Safavid—allusions to the empire ruled by present-day Iran
Non-Muslims	Infidels

SOURCE: RAND analysis, Twitter data from July 2014 to May 2015.

Themes of religion and belonging resonated strongly, as shown in overpresent terms such as #Mutual_ brotherly_support, *brother, the Sunni people,* and *the Muslims.* Other overpresent phrases included *thanks be to God, God is Great, for the pleasure of God, prayer,* #blessed_rule. This accompanied the widespread use of positive terms such as *good tidings* and *joy.* In reference to violent ISIS activities, users used noble phrases such as *lions of the Islamic State,* and *mujahideen,* and coopted the trappings of real states by using terms such as *army,* and *soldiers of the Caliphate.* The term *terrorists* was conspicuously absent.

This metacommunity frequently invoked the idea of a threat against Islam, and its references to enemies derogated them as varying categories of "other." See Table 3.2 for terms ISIS supporters apply to various Middle East actors. The treatment of rival Syrian rebel groups was mixed.[9]

Sunni States Distinct Messaging and Themes

The fourth metacommunity, *Sunni States,* shown in red in Figure 3.2, was more fractured than the others (this unique structure is discussed further in the next chapter). While a few pockets staunchly supported ISIS, most constituents predominantly opposed ISIS. Most content consisted of opposition to ISIS from Sunnis who self-divided into groups according to country and nationality, interspersed with spam and bot-like activity.

Some of the spam tweets appeared to be anti-ISIS, while others merely hijacked popular IS-related hashtags to advertise unrelated services. Given the amount of spam that appeared, it was not always easy, when assessing community content and themes, to separate out the contributions of this spam from the more legitimate Twitter conversation.[10]

---

[9]   Popular tweets suggested that groups of Jabhat al-Nusra are pledging allegiance to the Islamic State. Others claim that Jabhat al-Nusra is slandering the Islamic State, and call it the foolish "Front of Julani." In contrast, tweets about the Free Syrian Army discredit it by claiming that it is collaborating with the "*Nusayri* regime" and "Crusader coalition."

[10]   Two of the most frequently repeated usernames were users who had likely been suspended for spamming or bot usage; one grew "3,245% more popular" in one hour, and another's name suggests a service for buying retweets. The conspicuous absence of "rt," the abbreviation for retweet that typically appears at the beginning of retweets, in combination with the large swathes of identical tweets, suggests the influence of spamming bots. A typical irrelevant spam campaign consisted of 70,000 identical spam tweets that said, "sell retweets and

Saudi concerns about ISIS dominated at the metacommunity level, with hashtags such as #Daesh_plans_an_explosion_in_Riyadh and #The_arrest_of_a_Daesh_cell_in_Tamir, a Saudi city. Overpresent location names, such as Hafar al-Batin and #Gulf_Province, point to Saudi Arabia and the Gulf, as well as Egypt, Libya, and ISIS "provinces" in Iraq. Relevant repeated Twitter usernames included an account that seeks to "raise awareness" about Saudi political detainees and a Saudi-based TV channel. Leaders whose names were conspicuously overpresent were Sunni Saudi imams Mohamad al-Arefe, Saudi al-Shuraim, and Abdul Rahman al-Sudais, in addition to Fayes al-Maliki, a Saudi actor and public ambassador to the Gulf. Other state institutions mentioned positively included #Ministry_of_the_Interior and the #Border_Guard. A sense of collective defense and identity was strong, with phrases such as *appoint and preserve the men of the security and military*, *preserve the nation*, *our nations*, *our homeland*, and *our security*.

This community denounced ISIS and enemies using secular terms such as *terrorists*, *their explosions*, and *crimes*, as well as religiously tinged words and phrases: *with sins*, *disbelieves*, and *fitna*. This last term refers to sectarian discord and dangerous chaos, and, in the Arab world, it is frequently invoked as the threatening alternative to the stability that autocratic governments provide. Users also used positive words with religious connotations, such as *prayer*, *glory*, *Ramadan*, *praise*, *the prophet*, as well as *truth*, *beginning*, and *love*.

Other resonant themes included U.S. untrustworthiness and ISIS collusion with Iran, as in the hashtag #Daesh_and_Iran_are_against_Saudi_Arabia. Mistrust of the United States was expressed through the hashtag #campaign_to_uncover_the_crimes_of_America. Another overpresent term was *September 11th*, which was used as in the following tweet: "America achieved its many goals with lies about September 11 and will achieve its great goals with lies about Daesh." Other popular hashtags were pro-IS in origin, such as #support_the_accounts_of_the_supporters_after_deletion, and could indicate the presence of either actual ISIS supporters in this metacommunity or campaigns to hijack pro-IS hashtags.

Summary

In summary, we distilled the Arabic Twitter conversation surrounding ISIS into 36 distinct communities and ultimately into four major metacommunities. Lexical analysis shows that these groups appear to belong to Shia, Sunni, Syrian mujahideen, and ISIS supporters.

- The Shia metacommunity makes frequent references to Shia issues, is focused on Sunni/Shia divisions, and links ISIS to Saudi Arabia.
- The Syrian Mujahideen metacommunity represents Middle East–based Syrian mujahideen supporters who have mixed attitudes toward the Islamic State and generally negative attitudes toward the international coalition.

---

likes #Citizen_gives_his_wife_a_piece_of_land #Asian_injustice #My_first_Tweet #Easy_as_ease #Pray_for_the_Organization_of_Daesh." Other telling and overpresent phrases include *prices*, *cheaper*, *sex*, #sell_retweet, #sell_followers. Anti-IS spam also had clear themes of Saudi nationalism, with 25,000 identical tweets reading, "God preserve you, O Homeland, #Daesh, #Daesh_announces_the_caliphate, #Al-Qaeda_in_the_Arab_Peninsula, #Islamic_State, #State_of_the_Caliphate, #Saudi_Arabia." Similarly vast swaths of tweets denounced "the terrorists of Jabhat al-Nusra," while cheering on "men of our security at all borders" and specifically the Saudi Emergency Forces.

- The ISIS Supporter metacommunity frequently invokes threats against Islam, highlights positive themes that include religion, belonging, and positive terms, and uses a variety of insults and derogatory terms toward their enemies. Members also appear to adhere to good social media strategy by actively encouraging fellow supporters to "spread," "disseminate," and "link" messages to expand their reach and impact.
- The Sunni metacommunity is highly fractured in comparison with other metacommunities; resonant themes are very different within the various Sunni subcommunities and appear to align with different Middle East nation states.

CHAPTER FOUR

ISIS Debate: Community Structure

While characterizing the content of the ISIS debate is very important to designing effective countermessaging strategies, understanding the structure of the debate—which communities are interacting and to what extent they talk to each other—is vital for determining where those strategies should be targeted. Communities that have lots of ties with others in the network can be particularly useful for influencing the largest number of participants with minimal effort. Other communities can occupy bridge or connector positions, serving as the unique conduit between communities. In this chapter we discuss the connections between the communities participating in the online ISIS debate and identify prominent structural elements.

In viewing the ISIS Twitter debate as a network, we highlight the number and direction of mentions between user accounts. However, with a network of over 770,000 user accounts and 3.3 million mentions, it is very difficult to discern any internal structure. Instead of relying on the user account network, we examine the community network, where each node in the network represents an entire community of user accounts, and the edges between communities aggregate the mentions between users in those respective communities. Figure 4.1 depicts the largest communities in the network and their connections.

Visualizing the network this way and removing the large number of "spoke" communities (clearly visible in Figure 3.2), we see that the core of the community network comprises several communities with a large number of connections between them, representing all four of the metacommunities. To make this structure more clear, we focus on the relative strength of the edges between communities, showing only the highest-density connections in Figure 4.2.

Removing the noise and focusing on only the relatively highest-density connections between communities, as we do in Figure 4.1, reveals several key structural elements. As we might expect from sectarian divisions, the Shia metacommunity is far from the ISIS Supporter metacommunity, connected to it only through the Syrian Mujahideen metacommunity and a few Sunni communities. Figure 4.2 highlights the way the Syrian Mujahideen metacommunity appears to be particularly important to this core network, due to its position between ISIS supporters and potentially more moderate Sunni communities. It is possible that it could serve as an important influencer node to sway ISIS supporters with countermessaging. Finally, one community in particular stands out for its relatively large amount of interaction with the ISIS Supporter metacommunity. Examining the content of its messages (see Appendix C for details), we determined that this community consists of a relatively small number of virulent ISIS opponents, mentioning and insulting ISIS supporters in their tweets. This community is labeled *ISIS Provocateurs* in Figure 4.2. While it is unlikely that hurling insults will change the minds of any committed ISIS supporters, there is a fair amount of response from the pro-ISIS

Figure 4.1
Connections Between Metacommunities

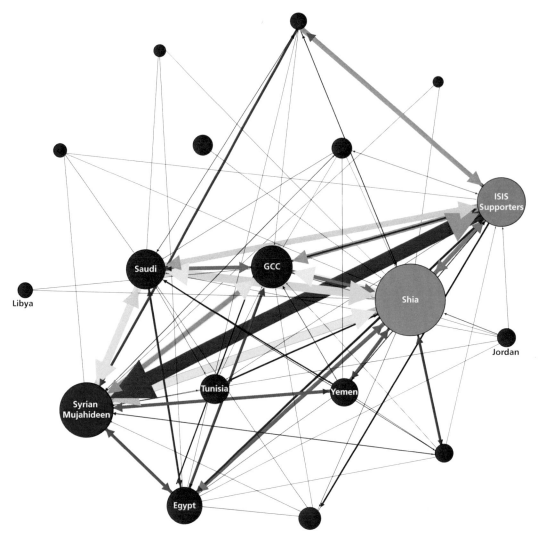

SOURCE: RAND analysis, Twitter data from July 2014 to May 2015.
NOTE: In this figure each node represents a community, with the size of the node indicating the size of the community. Red nodes indicate membership in the Sunni metacommunity. Edge thickness and color intensity (gray to red) indicate the number and direction of mentions between communities. Given resource constraints, not all communities could be examined with lexical analysis; unexplored communities appear without a label. GCC = Gulf Cooperation Council.
RAND RR1328-4.1

community, perhaps resulting in time spent responding to insults instead of spreading propaganda or recruiting.

Sunni Community Structure

One of the key differences between the four metacommunities shown in Figure 3.2 is their structure. While the Syrian Mujahideen, Shia, and ISIS Supporter metacommunities have a very clear hub and spoke (or star) structure with a central large community and many smaller

Figure 4.2
High-Density Connections Between Metacommunities

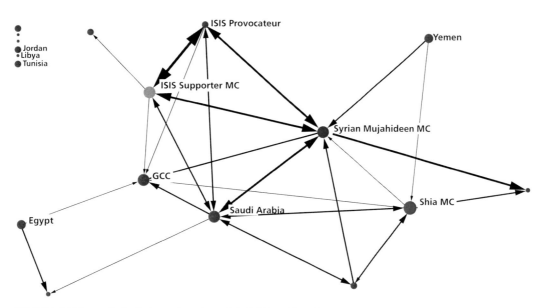

SOURCE: RAND analysis, Twitter data from July 2014 to May 2015.
NOTE: This figure illustrates the higher-density connections between metacommunities (more than 2,000 mentions), highlighting those that are higher in intensity, relative to community size. Node size represents the size of the community. Red nodes indicate membership in the Sunni metacommunity. Given resource constraints, not all communities could be examined with lexical analysis; unexplored communities appear without a label. MC = metacommunity.

RAND *RR1328-4.2*

connected communities, the Sunni metacommunity is highly fractured between several large communities. We characterized seven of these communities using lexical analysis, comparing actual frequencies of words in the target community against expected frequencies from the baseline of all other communities in the Sunni metacommunity. These seven communities represent 60 percent of the users, 51 percent of the tweets, and 52 percent of the words from the Sunni metacommunity (Table 4.1).

These communities and the connections between them are shown in Figure 4.3. From this figure we can see that the Egypt, Gulf, and Saudi communities form the core of the Sunni metacommunity, with Yemen and Tunisia as second-tier communities and Libya and Jordan on the periphery.[1]

Plotting the active users in each Sunni community by day (Figure 4.4), we see a similar pattern of activity across the communities. Jordan, Saudi Arabia, and the Gulf States, and, to a lesser extent, Egypt, are particularly similar in their activity patterns.

Examining the users in each community more closely according to their individual use of the Arabic terms for *Islamic State* and *Daesh*, we see that it is possible that the similarity in activity across communities is a reflection of the communities' affiliations, either pro- or anti-ISIS. In particular, the Saudi Arabia, Jordan, and Egypt communities have very similar compositions.

---

[1]   As with the metacommunities, the Sunni communities were first identified via network analysis and then characterized using lexical analysis. See Appendix C for more details. Note that due to project constraints, we characterized only some of the Sunni communities.

Table 4.1
Sunni Communities Composition

Community Label	Users	Tweets	Words	Spam (%)
GCC	59,116	2,397,777	36,920,811	20
Saudi Arabia	55,439	3,478,777	57,639,937	21
Egypt	47,410	2,115,216	36,549,200	5
Tunisia	34,899	508,279	8,061,090	10
Yemen	30,247	1,071,867	17,313,414	10
Libya	8,298	258,401	4,273,809	0
Jordan	13,381	398,148	6,502,702	0
Total, examined communities	227,111	9,571,916	156,484,452	16
Total, Sunni States	379,778	18,638,101	299,322,234	11

SOURCE: RAND analysis, Twitter data from July 2014 to May 2015.

Despite this similarity, however, each Sunni community has unique messaging themes and resonant topics, as determined by our lexical analysis and shown in Table 4.2. In particular, it is interesting to note that while the Saudi Arabian community appears to have few ISIS supporters according to the "Islamic State" versus "Daesh" measure, lexical analysis of key themes reveals that pro-ISIS content is, in fact, dominant (Table 4.3). For instance, while the words *Daesh* and *dens* in one hashtag popular in this community, #The_Emirates_blow_up_the_dens_of_Daesh, suggest support for this anti-ISIS action, most of the tweets using the hashtag in this community were disapproving of or concerned about associated civilian casualties. ISIS supporters may sometimes use *Daesh* hashtags to push their content onto the screens of ISIS opponents or those who are undecided and therefore "hijack" these terms or hashtags. While the lexical analysis preformed on users who predominantly used *Islamic State* versus those who used *Daesh* terms confirmed their usefulness as a rough discriminant for support and opposition, this example highlights the need to combine different analytic approaches

Table 4.2
Sunni Communities' Stance Toward ISIS

Community	% Daesh	% *ISIS*	% Both	% Neither
Yemen	48.8	30.5	8.7	12.4
ISIS Provocateurs	52.5	14.5	6.7	26.3
GCC	75.5	7.9	5.0	11.6
Libya	78.3	7.0	3.4	11.2
Saudi Arabia	79.8	6.3	4.7	9.3
Jordan	80.7	5.3	3.8	10.3
Egypt	81.4	5.4	4.6	8.6
Tunisia	81.1	2.3	1.7	15.0

SOURCE: RAND analysis, Twitter data from July 2014 to May 2015.

Figure 4.3
Sunni Communities Structure

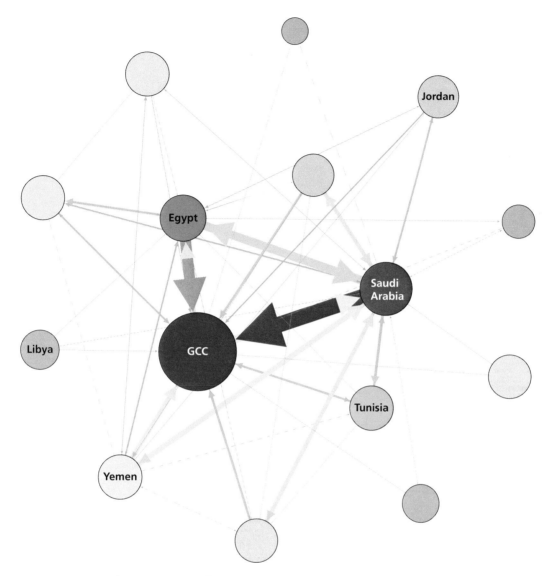

SOURCE: RAND analysis, Twitter data from July 2014 to May 2015.
NOTE: Node size represents the size of the community, and node color its betweenness centrality. Only
the communities analyzed lexically are labeled.
RAND *RR1328-4.3*

to ensure that the larger picture is understood. See Appendix C for more details on these key themes for each community.

The Sunni communities also vary in terms of their geographic dispersion, with a couple (Libya and Jordan) very concentrated in one geographic area, while others are more global, perhaps representing migrant communities around the world. The two maps in Figure 4.5 show the geotagged tweets belonging to each community, a small percentage of the total tweet volume but indicative of the geographic spread of the various communities. Note that due to the low percentage of geotagged tweets, we did not use this analysis to draw specific conclu-

Figure 4.4
Sunni Communities Active Users (per Day)

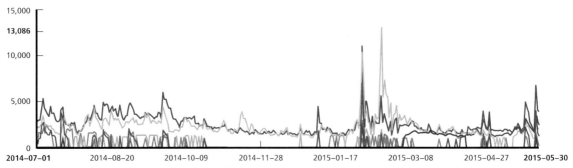

SOURCE: RAND analysis, Twitter data from July 2014 to May 2015.
NOTE: Limited to communities exceeding a minimum threshold of 100 active users per day. Line colors indicate different Sunni communities.
RAND *RR1328-4.4*

Table 4.3
Sunni Communities' Key Message Themes

Sunni Community	Message Themes
Saudi Arabia	ISIS support and expansion in Saudi Arabia threats to Islam posed by Iranian Shiism, secular nationalism, international community
Egypt	nationalism ISIS opposition mistrust of Brotherhood frustration with U.S. policies
Jordan	nationalism Moath al-Kasabeh support for international air campaign
Libya	nationalism ISIS opposition distrust of Libyan politicians, militants, and West
Yemen	ISIS support criticism of Kingdom of Saudi Arabia intervention
ISIS Provocateurs	insults
Tunisia	spam (pro- and anti-ISIS, selling unrelated services) and bots using hashtags related to Tunisia
GCC	mostly anti-ISIS spam

SOURCE: RAND analysis, Twitter data from July 2014 to May 2015.

sions. Instead, we used it to indicate where further analysis of particular communities was needed, such as in the Libyan and Jordanian communities.

Figure 4.5
Geospatial Analysis of Sunni Communities

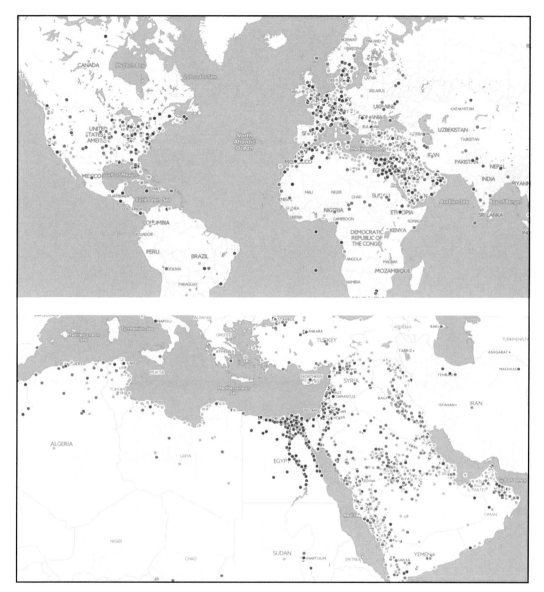

SOURCE: RAND analysis, Twitter data from July 2014 to May 2015.
NOTE: Node color indicates community membership, as determined by network analysis. Different colors indicate distinct communities.

RAND *RR1328-3.2*

Summary

In summary, we conducted social network analysis to examine the relationship between different Twitter communities. We found that the core of the Syrian Mujahideen metacommunity serves an important connection between otherwise disconnected groups that include the Shia metacommunity, some Sunni communities, and the ISIS Supporter metacommunity. It is thus possible that individuals within the Syrian Mujahideen metacommunity could serve as influencers of ISIS supporters and connect ISIS opponents together. Our analysis also examined the makeup of the Sunni metacommunity and found that Egyptian, Saudi Arabian, and GCC subcommunities serve as core components. In most of these communities, ISIS opponents far outnumber ISIS supporters. The exception is the Yemeni community, which has the highest percentage of ISIS supporters and is sharply divided between ISIS supporters and opponents.

CHAPTER FIVE

Recommendations and Implications

Our findings demonstrate that Arabic-language ISIS opponents vastly outnumber ISIS supporters. Indeed, this ratio grows even larger when one considers the average numbers of tweeters per day. According to our analysis, there were an average of 20,000 ISIS opponents tweeting on a daily basis, in comparison with approximately 2,000 ISIS supporters. This effectively raises the ratio to 10:1.

While ISIS supporters are outnumbered, it is clear that they are more active than ISIS opponents, as they produce 150 percent of opponents' number of tweets a day. These results suggest that ISIS supporters are more energized than their opponent counterparts. However, more than this, lexical analysis of the ISIS Supporters metacommunity demonstrates that ISIS supporters more actively adhere to good social media strategy by actively encouraging fellow supporters to "spread," "disseminate," and "link" messages to expand their reach and impact.

The great abundance of ISIS opponents already active on Twitter suggests the core ingredients for an effective grassroots anti-ISIS campaign already exist. However, ISIS opponents may need additional help to enhance the effectiveness and reach of their messaging. While it is beyond the scope of this paper to provide a full strategy for doing so, there are some suggestions we can make. The commercial marketing industry, for example, is cutting new ground by refining approaches for working with and empowering influencers or third-party validators. It is well known, for example, that Pabst Blue Ribbon beer received its second life in part because of the company's strategic engagement with hipsters in Portland (Walker, 2003). Common tactics used in influencer engagement strategies include identifying and working with potentially influential persons and helping them enhance their communication skills via social media training and providing them access to curated sources of content that are highly sharable (Phillips et al., 2010; Rand, 2013; and Wright, 2014, for example). It is also possible to give them access to experiences that help them tell their story. A potential example of this might be allowing influencers an opportunity to interview an ISIS dropout or an anti-ISIS mujahideen fighter, which in turn gives them great content to share with their audiences. Approaches to influence marketing are varied, and many other tactics are available. The United States and the international community already provide training in social media to select civil society members in the Muslim world, and such programs could be expanded and strengthened to provide a more robust effort to expand the voice of ISIS opponents.

ISIS Suffered a Significant Drop in Tweeted Support; Atrocities and Suspensions May Prove a Vulnerability for ISIS

Our analysis shows a clear decline in the number of ISIS supporters tweeting on a daily basis. This decline begins in early April 2015, when approximately 2,000 supporters were tweeting per day, to the end of May, when that number declined to approximately 1,300. At the same time, ISIS opponents appeared emboldened, with a May increase in daily tweeters from 20,000 to 30,000 or 40,000. At the end of our data collection period, the ratio of daily tweeting ISIS opponents to supporters reached 30:1.

Without collecting additional data, it is impossible to know whether this trend was sustained in June 2015 and beyond. However, several factors may explain this trend. First, the reduction may be a result of the Twitter suspension campaign. That campaign began in the spring of 2015 and was credited with 10,000 Twitter suspensions on April 4, 2015 alone (Hall, 2015). Despite the ease of opening new accounts, the suspension campaign likely disrupted ISIS Twitter communications.

Second, the trend may partly be an indication of reduced global support for ISIS. It is tantalizing to connect this trend with the Twittersphere reaction to the burning of the Jordanian pilot, Moath al-Kasabeh. This atrocity resulted in a temporary but massive spike in the number of tweeting ISIS opponents and a reduction in the number of tweeting ISIS supporters. Prior research also suggests that anti-ISIS tweets peak when ISIS human rights violations are publicly disseminated (Magdy, Darwish, and Weber, 2015). While there is a two-month time lag between the Jordanian pilot incident and the rise in daily tweeting ISIS opponents, it may be a precipitating factor.

Overall, these observations suggest several recommendations. First, it seems prudent for Twitter to continue its campaign of account suspensions. The campaign likely harasses ISIS Twitter users, forces them to lose valuable time reacquiring followers, and may ultimately push some to use social media channels far less public and accessible than Twitter.

Second, the use of highlighting ISIS atrocities should be thoroughly explored. The Twitter impact of the burning of the Jordanian pilot as well as previous findings suggesting a relation between ISIS atrocities and ISIS opposition on Twitter indicate that such atrocities may galvanize opponents (Magdy, Darish, and Weber, 2015). However, ISIS clearly uses ultraviolence as a key component of its brand, so a messaging strategy highlighting such actions risks playing into its hands (Winter, 2015).

It is evident when examining Figures 2.1 and 2.2 that the activity of ISIS supporters and opponents experiences abrupt spikes and troughs. A more systematic examination of the causes behind these spikes and troughs, such as ISIS atrocities, would be valuable.

The Arabic Community on Twitter Is Highly Fragmented, Split Along Sectarian and National Lines

This study used a series of community detection algorithms to identify groups of tightly connected Twitter users. The findings were noteworthy in that communities largely formed as a function of sectarian and national divisions. Beyond the Syrian Mujahideen and ISIS Supporters metacommunities, Shia and Sunni populations fell into their own separate communities. Furthermore, the Sunni metacommunity was uniquely composed of a host of smaller communities that, based on our examination of some of the most central communities, were organized around Middle East and North African nation-states. For example, using lexical analysis, we found that prominent themes in the group subsequently labeled "Egypt" included Egyptian nationalism and mistrust of the Muslim Brotherhood, as well as opposition to ISIS and frustration with U.S. policies. Likewise, common themes for the group subsequently labeled "Libya" included Libyan nationalism, distrust of Libyan politicians (and Libyan militants and the

West), and ISIS opposition. Nationalistic themes pervaded the Saudi Arabian, Jordanian, and Yemeni communities as well.

These observations (summarized in Table 5.1) have two implications for countermessaging efforts against ISIS. First, the tightly connected nature of users within each community indicates that viral messages are more likely to reverberate in and around these communities and less likely to reverberate between communities. Second, by virtue of the unique themes and messages detected in the discourse of these communities, it seems evident that messages will resonate differently across different communities. For example, nationalism is a prominent theme across nearly all examined Sunni communities. Thus, the use of Egyptian or Libyan nationalistic themes may provide a way to connect to those in the Egyptian and Libyan communities, respectively. Likewise, nearly all the subcommunities, with the exception of Jordan, expressed frustration and distrust with U.S. and Western policies that they believe are responsible for President Assad's continued hold on power. Attempts to connect to these communities by touting U.S. intervention against ISIS may prove unsuccessful.

Consequently, nations and organizations looking to countermessage ISIS on Twitter should tailor messages for and target them to specific communities. The specific data for this present report are likely too dated to support present or future information operations against ISIS, but the process outlined in this report, especially the use of community detection algorithms combined with a lexical analysis of narrative content and social network analysis, provides a repeatable methodology that practitioners can draw on to identify target audiences and inform outreach approaches.

The themes and messages identified for the ISIS support group may also prove helpful. In general, ISIS supporters focus on religious justification, belonging, the threat against Islam, and dehumanization of enemies. To the extent feasible, the counter-ISIS coalition should seek to target these themes in anti-ISIS messaging. Furthermore, messaging should seek to protect nonradicals from adopting these views.

Table 5.1
Summary: Sunni Communities' Prominent Themes

Sunni Community	Potential Message Themes
Saudi Arabia	ISIS support and expansion in Saudi Arabia
	threats to Islam posed by Iranian Shiism, secular nationalism, international community
Egypt	nationalism
	ISIS opposition
	mistrust of Brotherhood
	frustration with U.S. policies
Jordan	nationalism
	Moath al-Kasabeh
	support for international air campaign
Libya	nationalism
	ISIS opposition
	distrust of Libyan politicians, militants, and West
Yemen	ISIS support
	criticism of Kingdom of Saudi Arabia intervention

SOURCE: RAND analysis, Twitter data from July 2014 to May 2015.

Network Analysis Supports Efforts to Work with Key Influencers

Social media influence, especially influence on Twitter, requires more than just prolific messaging. Being connected to the right people and having the right people raise your profile by retweeting and mentioning content is as important, if not more so, than crafting just the right message. Unfortunately, Twitter represents a vast, complex, and very diverse community of users, so it is often quite difficult to find and connect to those "right people." Network analysis, especially when combined with lexical analysis as presented in this report, is a powerful tool that can quickly and relatively easily identify key influencers within a population.[1]

To influence ISIS supporters, it will be important for the international countermessaging coalition (that includes the U.S. Department of State, Military Information Support Operations personnel, and others) to work to improve the Syrian Mujahideen metacommunity's anti-ISIS messaging. This metacommunity's unique position within the overall Twitter network indicates that it has a role to play in connecting ISIS opponents to supporters. Moreover, to the extent that members of this community are considered credible Muslim voices and can speak to the themes that resonate with ISIS supporters, they have the largest potential to sway that population.

To influence and bolster ISIS opponents and sway the broad middle ground, it will be essential to identify and support key influencers within individual Sunni communities. As evidenced by the fractured structure within this community, a single message theme will not suffice. Tailored messages like those described previously will need to be crafted and spread by influencers within each community. Network analysis performed at the user-account level can help identify these influencers, who could then be provided with social media training and other support, through nongovernmental and other organizations if direct U.S. support is not feasible or desired.

Summary of Recommendations

- Research institutions should continue to use the model of *Daesh* versus *Islamic State* for ISIS to gauge worldwide activity of ISIS supporters and opponents. The U.S. government may use such models to test the impact of anti-ISIS programs.
- ISIS opponents are plentiful but may require assistance from the U.S. State Department, in the form of social media trainings and other engagements, to enhance the effectiveness and reach of their messaging.[2] Of course, with al-Qa'ida and its affiliates counted among the ISIS opponents, care will have to be taken in selecting those suitable to train and empower.
- Twitter should continue its campaign of account suspensions: This campaign likely harasses ISIS Twitter users, forces them to lose valuable time reacquiring followers, and

---

[1]   We caveat this by stating that social media influencers do not necessarily have outsize influence on the real, offline world. However, social media influencers are a very valuable resource to quickly reach a connected, large population and should be leveraged as such.

[2]   The United States and the international community already provide training in social media to select civil society members in the Muslim world, and such programs could be expanded and strengthened to provide a more robust effort to amplify the voice of ISIS opponents.

may ultimately push some to use social media channels far less public and accessible than Twitter.

- U.S. military Information Support Operations planners, as well as State Department messengers, should continue to highlight ISIS atrocities. The Twitter impact of the burning of the Jordanian pilot as well as previous findings suggesting a relation between ISIS atrocities and ISIS opposition on Twitter indicate that such atrocities may galvanize opponents. Note, however, ISIS clearly uses ultraviolence as a key component of its brand, so a messaging strategy highlighting such actions risks playing into its hands (Winter, 2015). A more systematic examination of the causes behind spikes and troughs in Twitter activity of ISIS supporters and opponents would be valuable.
- Nations and organizations (such as U.S. military and State Department messengers) looking to countermessage ISIS on Twitter should tailor messages for and target them to specific communities: The ISIS Twitter universe is highly fragmented and consists of different communities that care about different topics. Countermessaging should take this into account with tailored communications to different communities.

Twitter Search

We used RAND's 2014–2015 contract with the social media data aggregator DataSift to search the entire historical Twitter fire hose for tweets that referenced ISIS. The specific search terms we used, including common grammatical variations, are shown in Table A.1.

Note that only the Arabic terms, not their English translations, were included in the query. We searched for tweets with the search terms outlined above from July 1, 2014, to April 30, 2015, as shown in the Curated Stream Definition Language (CSDL) code below.

```
{
    "common":
    {

        "startTimeGMT": "5/1/2015 00:00:00",
        "endTimeGMT": "6/1/2015 00:00:00",
        "sources": ["Twitter"],
    return {
```
interaction.content contains_any "الدَّولة الإسلامية، الدولة الإسلامية، الدولة الاسلامية، الدوله الإسلامية، الدوله الاسلامية، دولة الإسلام، دوله الاسلام، دولة الاسلام، دولة الخلافة، دوله الخلافه، دولة الخلافه، الخلافة الإسلامية، الخلافة الاسلامية، دولة الخلافة الإسلامية، دولة الخلافة الاسلامية، الدولة الإسلاميّة، الدولة _ الإسلاميّة، داعش،الداعش، داعش، الداعشي، داعشي، الداعشية، الداعشية، داعشيه، الداعشيه، دواعش، الدواعش، داعشيين، الداعشيين، داعشيون، الداعشيون"

OR

Twitter.hashtags contains_any "الدولة _ الإسلامية، الدولة _ الاسلامية، دولة _ الإسلام، دولة _ الاسلام، دولة _ الخلافة، الخلافة، الخلافة _ الإسلامية، الخلافة _ الاسلامية، دولة _ الخلافة _ الإسلامية، تنظيم _ داعش"
```
    }

}
```

Since our search terms were all in Arabic, most of the tweets were also in Arabic, although a few were in English or other languages with the Arabic terms. The data returned include the content of the tweet itself, the username and account number of the user who posted it, any public profile information the user may have had at the time, and associated metadata like time, location, platform used, etc. Note that these data include retweets as well as original tweets.

Table A.1
Twitter Search Terms

Islamic State Search Terms		Daesh Search Terms	
الدولة الإسلامية	The Islamic State	داعش	Daesh
الدولة الإسلامية	The islamic State	الداعش	the Daesh
الدولة _ الإسلامية	The islamic state	داعشي	Daeshi
الدولة _ الإسلامية	#The_Islamic_State	الداعشي	the Daeshi
الدولة _ الاسلامية	#The_islamic_State	داعشية	Daeshi [f]
دولة _ الإسلام	#State_of_Islam	الداعشية	the Daeshi [f]
دولة _ الاسلام	#State_of_islam	داعشيه	Daeshi [f]
دولة الإسلام	State of Islam	الداعشيه	the Daeshi [f]
دولة الاسلام	State of islam	دواعش	Daeshis
دولة _ الخلافة	#State_of_the_Caliphate	الدواعش	the Daeshis
دولة الخلافة	State of the Caliphate	داعشيين	Daeshis [accusative case]
دولة الخلافه	State of the caliphate	الداعشيين	the Daeshis [accusative case]
الخلافة _ الإسلامية	#The_Islamic_Caliphate	داعشيون	Daeshis [subjective case]
الخلافة الإسلامية	The Islamic Caliphate	الداعشيون	the Daeshis [subjective case]
الخلافة الاسلامية	The islamic Caliphate	تنظيم _ داعش	#The_Organization_of_Daesh
دولة _ الخلافة _ الإسلامية	#State_of_the_Islamic_Caliphate	الدولة _ الإسلامية في _ العراق _ والشآم	#The_Islamic_State_in_Iraq_and_Syria
دولة الخلافة الإسلامية	State of the Islamic Caliphate		
دولة الخلافة الاسلامية	State of the islamic Caliphate		
الدّولة الإسلامية	The Islamic State (with diacritics)		

Analytic Methods

Lexical Analysis

We used RAND-Lex, an internally developed lexical analysis software program, to perform comparative lexical analyses on corpora of tweets. RAND-Lex works by comparing the proportional frequencies of words in a target corpus against the proportional frequencies of the same words in a baseline corpus. The log likelihood calculation for a keyword, shown in the equation below, is a function of the actual frequency of the word in the target corpus compared with the frequency of the word that would be expected in the baseline corpus and indicates how conspicuous the overpresence or underpresence of that keyword in the target corpus is.

$$L = 2 \cdot \left(f_t \cdot \log \frac{f_t}{N_t \cdot (f_t + f_b) \cdot N_T^{-1}} + f_b \cdot \log \frac{f_b}{N_b \cdot (f_t + f_b) \cdot N_T^{-1}} \right)$$

f_t	Number of times the word appears in the target corpus
f_b	Number of times the word appears in the baseline corpus
N_t	Number of words in the target corpus
N_b	Number of words in the baseline corpus
N_T	Total number of words in both the target and the baseline corpus.

Log likelihood–based frequency analysis of keywords has an established literature on its use in corpora comparison (Scott, 1996, 2001; Hardy, 2007; Kenny, 2014). Some lexical analysis compares a specialized target corpus with a vast baseline corpus designed to be representative of general or typical language use; other lexical analysis, including the analysis in this study, instead compares one specialized corpus (in this case, tweets) to another specialized corpus (Rayson and Garside, 2002). This study utilized the second method to throw the tweet corpora into starker relief; Arabic tweets praising ISIS have many distinctive words in common with Arabic tweets condemning ISIS, when contrasted with generic, formal Arabic as used in newspapers. While comparing one specialized corpus to another specialized corpus may obscure ways in which both corpora differ from general language use, it also prioritizes and highlights differences between the two corpora that might otherwise go unnoticed.

To identify keywords, we employed a frequency cut-off of five occurrences (log likelihood keyness scores are significant at 6.63). Log likelihood scores, applied to these keywords, prioritized them by distinctiveness. The log likelihood calculations for all keywords analyzed exceeded 2,000, suggesting very specialized, distinctive language. Using RAND-Lex, we also identified collocates, sequences of words that co-occur more often than would be predicted by chance; these consist of either bigrams, which are word pairs, or trigrams, which consist of three co-occurring words. All collocates included in the community analyses were among the 200 most frequent bigrams or trigrams for each corpus. In this analysis we employed a frequency cut-off of ten occurrences and a point-wise mutual information (PMI) score of 3 or greater.

We performed three separate sets of lexical analyses. The first set sought to validate the use of terms *Islamic State* and *Daesh* (in Arabic) as rough predictors of support or opposition to ISIS. Out of our entire database of tweets, we constructed two samples to compare against each other. The *Islamic State* sample consisted of all tweets from all users in our database for whom the following condition applies: More than 80 percent of that user's tweets had one of the *Islamic State* phrases in it. This numbered 4 million tweets with 67 million words. The *Daesh* sample consisted of all tweets from all users in our database for whom the following condition applies: More than 80 percent of that user's tweets had one of the *Daesh* phrases in it. This numbered 18 million tweets, with 316 million words. The size of the two samples combined was 23 million tweets with 383 million words. Keywords included in the analysis had log likelihood calculations over 16,000, and collocates included in the analysis were among the most frequently used 500 bigrams or trigrams in each community.

The second set of lexical analyses characterized the four metacommunities by comparing actual frequencies of words in the target metacommunity against expected frequencies from the baseline of all of the other metacommunities (Table B.1). For instance, MC1 (subsequently labeled Syrian Mujahideen) was analyzed by treating MC1 as the target corpus and combining MC0 (Shia), MC2 (ISIS Supporters), and MC3 (Sunni States) to serve as the baseline corpus. For the analysis of the metacommunities, keywords included had log likelihood calculations over 5,000. Collocates included in the analysis were among the most frequently used 200 bigrams or trigrams in each community and were all used at least 5,000 times.

The third set of lexical analyses characterized seven communities from the Sunni States metacommunity, by comparing actual frequencies of words in the target community against expected frequencies from the baseline of all other communities in the Sunni metacommunity. The seven communities analyzed were chosen on the following basis. The first five communities analyzed were the five communities in the metacommunity with the largest number of users: GCC, Saudi Arabia, Egypt, Tunisia, and Yemen (C56, C23, C59, C1683, and C579, respectively). The last two communities, Libya (C932) and Jordan (C204), were selected because geospatial analysis indicated that those two communities were distinctively present in those two countries. Collectively, these seven examined communities represented 60 percent of the users, 51 percent of the tweets, and 52 percent of the words from the Sunni States metacommunity. When analyzing the communities, keywords had log likelihood calculations over 2,000. Col-

Table B.1
Breakdown of Metacommunities

Metacommunity Label	Users (%)	Tweets (%)	Words (%)
Shia	18	15	16
Syrian Mujahideen	12	12	13
ISIS Supporters	11	19	18
Sunni States	59	55	53

locates included in the analysis were among the most frequently used 100 bigrams or trigrams in each community, and were all used at least 450 times.

Network Analysis

Social network analysis is a formal quantitative method for the study of social structure, the potentially complex network of relationships between people that might emerge in any number of settings: families, schools, religious groups, sports teams, or corporations. Emerging as a key technique in sociology in the 1950s, social network analysis is "grounded in systematic empirical data, draws heavily on graphic imagery, and relies on the use of mathematical and/ or computational models" (Freeman, 2004), and has since seen its techniques applied in fields as far ranging as political science to computer science and electrical engineering (Easley and Kleinberg, 2010; Jackson, 2010; Newman, 2010). Rather than looking at people with individual characteristics (commonly called *attribute data*), social network analysis shifts the focus to *relationship data*, using techniques and terminology from network theory (Wasserman and Faust, 1994; Scott, 2000; Borgatti, Everett, and Johnson, 2013).

Relationship Data

Network analysis uses relational data to generate metrics that identify key nodes and network characteristics as well as visualizations, which illustrate network shape and organization. At a basic level, the required data for network analysis consist of a set of actors and the presence or absence of a particular type of relationship between actors—collected into a *binary, symmetric* network, like the one shown in Table B.2 and Figure B.1.

At a more advanced level, information about relationship strength, relationship direction, or even multiple types of relationships among the set of actors is collected into a *weighted, directed* network or set of networks (sometimes called a *multigraph*). In an *undirected* or *symmetric* network, an *edge* or tie (or relationship) from X to Y implies an equal edge from Y to X (the relationship is symmetric), whereas in a *directed* network, an edge from X to Y does not imply that an equal edge exists from Y to X. In *weighted* or *valued* networks, edges have values representing the strength of the relationship between X and Y, while in unweighted, or *binary*, networks, edges take on values only of 1 or 0, indicating either the presence or absence of a relationship but not describing the strength of the relationship.

Table B.2
Sample Adjacency Matrix

	Alice	Bob	Eve
Alice		1	
Bob	1		1
Eve		1	

Figure B.1
Sample Network Graph

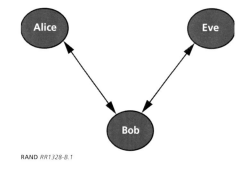

RAND RR1328-B.1

Relationship data are usually summarized in an *adjacency matrix*, as shown in Table B.2 for a simple binary symmetric network between Alice, Bob, and Eve. Relationship data can also be shown in a *network diagram*, sometimes called a *network graph* or simply *network*.[1] We show the corresponding network graph for Alice, Bob, and Eve's social network in Figure B.1. Network graphs represent nodes as circles or squares, with the relationships as lines connecting them. Arrowheads represent the direction of the relationship; undirected or binary networks often will not have arrowheads in the network graph. For most of the Twitter analyses in this report, the network is weighted and directed, with nodes representing Twitter accounts and edges representing the number of Twitter mentions.

Attribute data, data involving particular characteristics of nodes, can also be combined with relationship data for a richer picture of the network and interactions between actors. In the situation where the nodes in the network represent Twitter accounts, these sorts of data can include geographic location, stance toward ISIS, or anything uniquely related to the given node.

Network Metrics

Network metrics are formal quantitative calculations based on measures developed using graph theory,[2] calculated using relationship data, and forming the basis of social network analysis. Different network metrics exist for evaluating node- or individual-level data and network-wide data.

Node-level metrics are used to assess "network importance" or "network power." They are often useful for determining key players in a network and the relative ranking of other nodes. In many cases, the results obtained by calculating these metrics will agree with and provide support for the conclusions drawn in a qualitative assessment, but not in every case. It is important to remember that network metrics measure one type of importance—the amount of structural power a node has through its relationships to others in the network, which may or may not correspond to other definitions of power, such as economic wealth.

The first and simplest metric is *degree*. Degree counts the number of edges, or ties, a given node has to other nodes. Nodes with more edges may have more advantage in the network; they have more access to other nodes and so can influence more members, spread information further, or call upon more of the resources in the network. For a directed network (where relationships are defined to have a direction, from one node to the other), we can calculate both the *in-degree* and *out-degree* of a given node, the number of incoming and outgoing edges, respectively, while for symmetric networks, we calculate only *degree*. For valued or weighted networks, *weighted degree* is calculated using the sum of all edge weights incident upon a node, accounting for relationship strength, while *unweighted* or *binary degree* just counts the number of edges incident upon a node, ignoring relationship strength.

The second metric we consider is *betweenness centrality*, as defined by Freeman (Freeman, 1977), which measures nodes' brokerage power. Betweenness centrality counts the number of pairs of other nodes a given node is between. For example, say individual A is connected to individual B, who is connected to individual C (A-B-C). If B wants to communicate with either A or C, it can easily do so. However, if A or C wish to communicate with each other,

---

[1]   Older literature will refer to social network diagrams as *sociograms*.

[2]   We do not go into the details of graph theory relevant to social network analysis here, but interested readers can refer to Wasserman and Faust (1994), and Newman (2010).

they must go through B. Thus, B gains power by being able to broker contacts between the other nodes, or could even prevent communications and isolate other nodes. If alternative paths existed between A and C, say through another node D, B's power would correspondingly decrease. Note that betweenness is calculated the same way for both directed and undirected networks, as it depends on the path lengths between pairs of nodes, which could be directed or undirected, but edges are assumed to be unweighted (binary).

Degree and betweenness centrality present two different ways to measure the importance or power of each node in a given network. Nodes that score high in both measures can be very powerful nodes, while those that score high in only one have distinct roles (such as a node that has very high betweenness through connecting otherwise-disconnected parts of the network, playing a broker role). Each is a different, useful way of looking at power and position within a network. Of course, other network metrics for assessing network power also exist, including eigenvector centrality, flow centrality, closeness centrality, and more.[3]

Evaluating Network Structure

Density is a basic network-level metric that focuses on overall structure rather than the individual nodes within a network. At a basic level, for a binary network, *network density* is the number of ties that are present divided by the number of pairs—the proportion of all possible ties that are actually present in the network.[4] Networks that are dense (have a relatively high number of all possible ties) are more robust to failure—usually the removal of a few nodes will not make the network disconnected. Further, dense networks may be quicker and more efficient at spreading information among network members. Consider the children's game of telephone in which one player whispers a sentence to the next player, until the message is passed through all of the players and the final player repeats the message to all the players, in a format that is often quite different from the original sentence. If a message must pass through several people before everyone gets it, it could get lost or changed along the way. However, if the network is dense, many connections exist between all of the members, and the message can spread much more quickly and accurately.

Group density is another very useful network metric, which allows us to quantitatively assess how clustered a network is according to a particular grouping of nodes, as determined by some sort of categorical attribute data. For example, consider dividing a network into two groups, Group A and Group B (perhaps representing those using Twitter in support of or opposed to ISIS). Group density measures the relative number of ties within and between each group and is usually depicted in a *density matrix*, an example of which is shown in Table B.3. The numbers in each cell in the matrix represent the percentage of ties that exist out

---

[3]   Eigenvector centrality assigns relative centrality scores to every node based on the concept that connections to high-scoring nodes contribute more to the score of the node in question than equal connections to low-scoring nodes. Flow centrality is similar to betweenness centrality but assumes that actors will use all pathways that connect them, proportionally to the length of the pathways. The centrality score is then measured by the proportion of the entire flow between two actors (that is, through all of the pathways connecting them) that occurs on paths of which a given actor is a part (Hanneman and Riddle, 2005). Closeness centrality measures how close each node is to all other nodes in the network. This metric is calculated by first determining the "farness" of each node: the sum of lengths of the shortest paths from a given node to all other nodes (out-farness) or to a given node from all other nodes (in-farness). Closeness is then the reciprocal of farness.

[4]   In networks with weighted edges, density is defined as the average strength of ties across all possible ties. Density can also be calculated for directed networks, taking into account the direction of the edges (i.e., there could exist an edge from X to Y and one from Y to X, two total, whereas with a directed network, it can be only one edge).

Table B.3
Sample Density Matrix

	A	B
A	1	0.2
B	0.2	0.7

of total possible ties between members of the group. In this example, we have a fairly highly *clustered* network, meaning that each group has relatively high density within itself, but relatively low density between groups. In this case, every possible tie that could exist does exist between members of Group A (100 percent), but only 20 percent of ties that could exist do exist between Groups A and B. Group B is also fairly dense (70 percent of possible ties exist) but not as dense as Group A.[5]

Group density is a simple and quick way to get a basic idea of how clustered a network is by various group memberships. A highly clustered network is in some ways very robust and in others very vulnerable; each cluster on its own is robust to failure, but the network as a whole can likely be easily broken into separate components (one for each cluster). Nodes that connect different clusters often have high betweenness centrality and serve as "bridges" or brokers connecting dissimilar parts of the network and often-dissimilar nodes. These nodes gain power by occupying possible information choke points but are also highly vulnerable.

Density forms the basis for many clustering and community detection algorithms, including the one used in this report that is optimized for very large networks (Clauset, Newman, and Moore, 2004) and implemented in the Stanford Network Analysis Project (SNAP) library (Leskovec, 2014). In this algorithm, communities are defined as groups of nodes that have a higher density of edges within groups than between them. Good groupings have a high *modularity* score, while poor groupings that do not maximize within-group density have a low score.

Presenting Analytical Results Through Visualizations

Visualizations, presenting relationship data visually as a network graph like Figure B.1, are a key part of network analysis. Visualizations can provide an "at-a-glance" look at macrostructures, structurally important nodes, groupings of nodes, as well as the basic "who is connected to whom" information. Example structures include *cliques* (completely connected actors, everyone connected to everyone else), *pendants* (actors with only one tie to the rest of the network), *isolates* (actors with no ties to the rest of the network), and *components* (groups of actors connected to each other but without any connection to other groups).

Visualizations can also represent attribute data through the size, shape, or color of each node; for example, the size of each node in a particular network could denote level of influence on a focal actor, while the color could denote political affiliation. Such visual attributes can also represent the value of various node-level metrics, such as those described previously.

---

[5]   Another way of measuring the amount of clustering in a network is through Krackhardt and Stern's E-I index, which measures group embedding and takes into account the number of ties that might be expected to exist, given the size of the overall population and each subgroup. For further information regarding this metric, see Chapter 8 of Hanneman and Riddle (2005).

Finally, the *layout* of visualizations can also convey network information. Nodes can be placed randomly in a network graph (which usually does not convey any useful information); they can be placed in a circle, ordered by a particular attribute (such as level of influence); they can be grouped by a particular attribute (often useful for displaying ties between groups); or the layout can be optimized in a particular way to convey structural information. Different techniques exist for optimizing network layouts; the most common (and often the most informative) is the *spring embedding* algorithm. This algorithm uses iterative fitting to locate the nodes in such a way as to put those with the smallest path lengths to one another closest in the graph (Hanneman and Riddle, 2005). Basically, nodes with similar "network position" will be grouped closer together in the visualization, and distances between nodes in the graph can be interpreted as meaning nodes are more dissimilar. Most of the network visualizations in this paper use a variant of the spring embedding algorithm.

Sunni Community Analysis

In this appendix we detail the lexical and network analysis results from a deep dive into the content and structure of seven selected Sunni State communities.

GCC

This community (see Figure C.1), dominated by mostly anti-ISIS spam that focuses on Saudi Arabia and the other Gulf States, closely mimicked the lexical footprint of the larger Sunni States metacommunity. This is unsurprising; because this community had the highest tweet volume of any of the constituent communities of the Sunni States metacommunity, it naturally made the largest contribution to characterizing the metacommunity.

The leaders whose names were repeated most often by users in this community were Fayes al-Maliki, Saudi actor and public ambassador to the Gulf; and three Sunni Saudi clerics and imams: Mohamad al-Arefe, Saudi al-Shuraim, and Abdul Rahman al-Sudais. Routana Khali-jia, a UAE-based television channel, also featured prominently. Overpresent location names included Saudi Arabia, Riyadh, Dammam, Bahrain, the Gulf, and Egypt. The vast swaths of identical tweets matched those in the larger Sunni States metacommunity perfectly, with thousands of identical tweets reading "God preserve you, O Homeland, #Daesh, #Daesh_announces_the_caliphate, #Al-Qaeda_in_the_Arab_Peninsula, #Islamic_State, #State_of_the_Caliphate, #Saudi_Arabia." Many identical tweets referenced "the terrorists of Jabhat al-Nusra," encouraged the "men of our security at all borders," and praised the Saudi Emergency Forces.

Figure C.1
GCC Community Active Users (per Day)

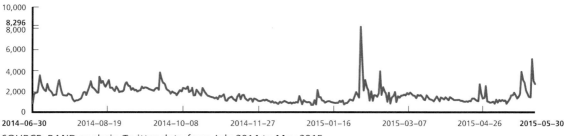

SOURCE: RAND analysis, Twitter data from July 2014 to May 2015.
RAND RR1328-C.1

There were, however, some overpresent pro-IS terms. These included "Remaining" (*Baqiya*), the first half of the ISIS motto, and the hashtag #Islamic_State_is_preparing_for_the_liberation_of_the_country_of_the_two_holy_mosques, which refers to Saudi Arabia.

The GCC community–mentions network, with 59,116 users, is shown in Figure C.2. This is the largest Sunni community we examined and is mostly anti-ISIS, with 75 percent of users regularly using the Arabic term *Daesh* and only 8 percent using *Islamic State*. It has a very classic core/periphery structure, with many highly connected users in the center of the network and many user "chains" (very common in Twitter mention networks) on the periphery. There are a few prominent and potentially influential pro-ISIS users, but the majority of the core is made up of ISIS opponents.

Figure C.2
GCC Community Network Representation

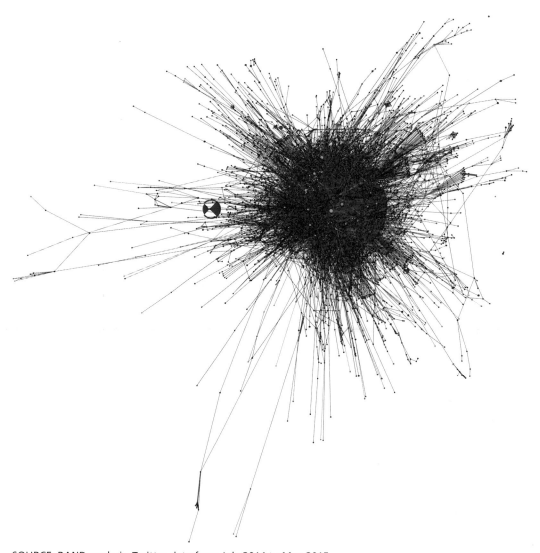

SOURCE: RAND analysis, Twitter data from July 2014 to May 2015.
NOTE: Node size indicates in-degree; color indicates stance (blue = anti-ISIS, red = pro-ISIS, green = both, gray = neither), as determined by use of *Daesh* versus *Islamic State*.
RAND *RR1328-C.2*

Egypt

This community (see Figure C.3) appeared to be composed primarily of Egyptians. Egyptian nationalism resonated strongly, as did opposition to ISIS, mistrust of the Muslim Brotherhood, and frustration with U.S. priorities in the region.

The community was clearly dominated by Egyptian users, as indicated by the proliferation of Egyptian colloquial terms and overpresence of terms such as *Egyptian*, *Egyptians*, and *Egypt*. Other distinctive location names included Sinai, Libya, Turkey, and Israel. Key figures were Fattah al-Sisi, the current president of Egypt, affiliated with the Egyptian military; and Mohamed Morsi, the ousted president of Egypt, affiliated with the Muslim Brotherhood. Distinctive institutions and organizations mentioned included "The Brotherhood," a reference to the Egyptian-origin Muslim Brotherhood; Ansar Beit al-Muqadis, the Egyptian terror group based in the Sinai Peninsula that has joined IS; Hamas, the Palestinian group based across the border from Egypt in the Palestinian territories; and Al-Azhar, Sunni Islam's most prestigious university, located in Cairo. "Egypt Today" (al-Masry al-Youm), an Egyptian news outlet, was also overpresent.

Stances suggested by the context in which these names were used included support for the current, President Sisi–led government, and opposition to ISIS and the Muslim Brotherhood. Users denounced ISIS members as *terrorists*; *Kharijites*, a derogatory term for Muslim extremists; and *the Salafis*. This last term negatively associates ISIS with the Muslim Brotherhood, as both organizations belong to the fundamentalist Salafi stream of Islamic thought.

Egyptian nationalism featured prominently. Nationalism was displayed with hashtags such as #News_of_Egypt, #Long_live_Egypt, #movement_of_our_nation, and #Egypt's_martyrs_in_Libya, and common phrases such as *the people* and *the army*. Members of this community also paid particular attention to the plight of Christians under IS; one tweet read, "Despite the threats of the terrorists of Daesh, O Lord, preserve the Christians in Iraq." Another popular hashtag suggested tensions with Qatar, which owns Muslim Brotherhood–friendly Al Jazeera Network: #Qatar_is_a_dirty_girl.

Negative but nuanced attitudes toward the United States emerged; conspicuous use of *America* and *Obama* evinced frustration with U.S. priorities and a sense that the U.S. activities in the region are both hypocritical and inscrutable. Some users insinuated that the United States is conspiring with the al-Sisi regime, such as in the following tweet: "Mathematical equations that even Einstein can't solve: The coup-regime is with America against Daesh, but with Daesh against the Muslim Brotherhood." Another read, "The Egyptian situation is seri-

Figure C.3
Egyptian Community Active Users (per Day)

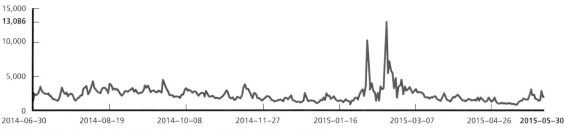

SOURCE: RAND analysis, Twitter data from July 2014 to May 2015.

ous, and known only to Sisi, the Brotherhood, Daesh, and America." Another excoriated the United States for caring about getting rid of ISIS but not the Assad regime: "Daesh slaughtering and burning a few people mobilized America and dozens of countries to make killing Daesh a priority; even though Bashar is destroying the homeland and displacing the people, America does not consider it to be a priority." Another read: "Obama lacks a clear strategy in the fight against Daesh using airstrikes."

Figure C.4 depicts the Egyptian community network, comprising 47,410 users, 81 percent of whom are anti-ISIS and only 5 percent pro-ISIS. Structurally, this network is interesting because it appears to have two major groups within it—one overwhelmingly anti-ISIS (bottom half of the network in the figure) and one more mixed (top half of the network, with the higher concentration of pro-ISIS and potentially neutral users). Further analysis would need to be performed to determine whether these two groups are lexically distinct, and what factors, if any, led to this split.

Figure C.4
Egyptian Community Network Representation

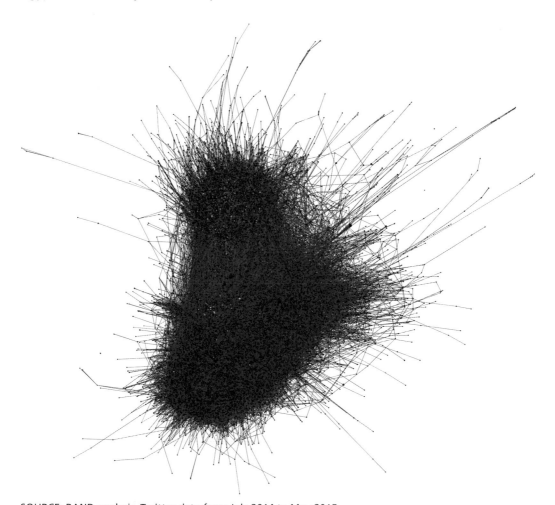

SOURCE: RAND analysis, Twitter data from July 2014 to May 2015.
NOTE: Node size indicates in-degree; color indicates stance (blue = anti-ISIS, red = pro-ISIS, green = both, gray = neither), as determined by use of *Daesh* versus *Islamic State*.
RAND *RR1328-C.4*

Saudi Arabia

This community (see Figure C.5) appeared to consist of ISIS supporters particularly focused on ISIS expansion to Saudi Arabia. Resonant themes included the threat to Sunni Islam imposed by Iranian Shiism, secular nationalism, Christianity, and the international community.

Support for ISIS was clear, due to hashtag campaigns such as #Remaining_and_Expanding (*Baqiya_wa_Tatamudud*), the ISIS motto, and #migration[*hijra*]_to_the_House_of_Islam_is_obligatory. ISIS official spokesperson Muhammad al-Adnani featured very prominently, along with popular hashtags like #al-Adnani_alerts_the_supporters_of_the_State and #So_they_kill_and_are_killed, the title of an Adnani audio address from March 2015. The names of two ISIS media outlets, Furqan Institute and al I'tisam Institute, were also overpresent, as was *The Brotherhood*, a reference to the Muslim Brotherhood. While the hashtag #The_Emirates_blow_up_the_dens_of_Daesh appears to support this anti-IS action, most of the tweets from this community appeared to disapprove or be concerned about civilian casualties. Apparently anti-IS terms and phrases included #Daesh_is_a_Brotherhood_plant, *the terrorism of Al Qaeda, Kharijites*, a derogatory term for Muslim extremists, and *dogs of fire*, frequently used to derogate ISIS members.

Desire for ISIS expansion to Saudi Arabia played a key role in this community, with popular hashtags such as #We_ask_the_caliph_to_invade_the_Gulf" (*al-Jazeera*); #The_State_to_the_edge_of_Arar, a Saudi city near the Iraqi border; and #The_Islamic_State_is_near_in_the_Arabian_Peninsula. Locations of particular interest to this community included ISIS provinces, the Gulf, Saudi Arabia, Arar, Ayn al-Islam, and Kobani.

The message that Sunni Islam was under attack by Iranian Shiism, secular nationalism, Christianity, and the international community was resonant in this community. Users denounced nationalism as un-Islamic with the hashtag #break_the_national_idol. The threat of secularism and Christianity was suggested by the hashtag #the_Muslims_of_Lebanon_will_Christianize_you. The community also invoked a sectarian threat to Sunni Islam by emphasizing the Iranian and Huthi Shia threats and using derogatory terms for Iranians, such as *the Safavids*, and *the Magis*. The sense of threat from the international community and the United States emerged in phrases and terms such as #campaign_to_uncover_the_crimes_of_America, *September 11*, and #second_mesage_to_America.

The Saudi community depicted in Figure C.6 represents 55,439 users, 80 percent of whom regularly use the term *Daesh* and thus, in theory, are anti-ISIS. However, the lexical analysis preceding indicates a different story, and the structure of the network could provide an explanation. This network has a similar though more complicated structure to that of the Egyptian

Figure C.5
Saudi Community Active Users (per Day)

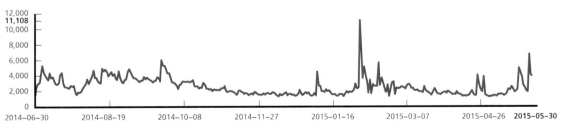

SOURCE: RAND analysis, Twitter data from July 2014 to May 2015.

RAND RR1328-C.5

Figure C.6
Saudi Community Network Representation

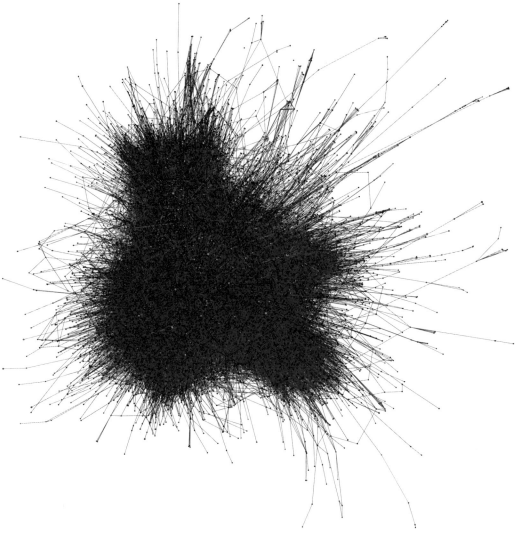

SOURCE: RAND analysis, Twitter data from July 2014 to May 2015.
NOTE: Node size indicates in-degree; color indicates stance (blue = anti-ISIS, red = pro-ISIS, green = both, gray = neither), as determined by use of *Daesh* versus *Islamic State*.
RAND *RR1328-C.6*

community, with a blurrier line between the anti-ISIS and more mixed groups of users. Within that more mixed group, users that are pro-ISIS or potentially neutral (shown in red and green, respectively) are very prominent. Not only are they prolific (indicated by the results of the lexical analysis), but they also occupy important network positions and thus are potentially influential within the Saudi Twitter community.

Tunisia

This community (see Figure C.7) was dominated by spam and bot-like activity that leveraged hashtags related to IS, including the ISIS attack on the Bardo Museum in Tunisia.

Figure C.7
Tunisian Community Active Users (per Day)

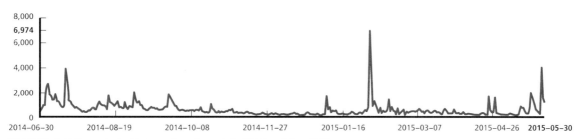

SOURCE: RAND analysis, Twitter data from July 2014 to May 2015.
RAND RR1328-C.7

The Tunisia-relevant hashtags and phrases were *Tunisia*, #Tunisia_is_the_den_of_the_monotheists, #Battle_of_the_Bardo_Museum, #Bardo_Museum, #Tunis_Caliphate, #battle_of_Tunisia. The IS-relevant hashtags and phrases that did not reference Tunisia were *the Houthis*, #campaign_to_delete_sectarian_followers, #message_from_the_Saudi_people_

Figure C.8
Tunisian Community Network Representation

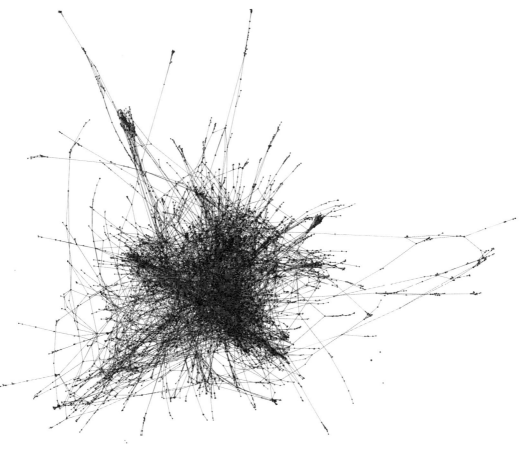

SOURCE: RAND analysis, Twitter data from July 2014 to May 2015.
NOTE: Node size indicates in-degree; color indicates stance (blue = anti-ISIS, red = pro-ISIS, green = both, gray = neither), as determined by use of *Daesh* versus *Islamic State*.
RAND RR1328-C.8

to_Daesh, #what_is_to_be_done_if_Daesh_enters_Saudi_Arabia, #Daesh_burns_the_Jor-danian_pilot, and *take the oath of allegiance to the caliph.*

This seemingly random mix of pro-IS and anti-IS messages suggests that the coordinator of the spam campaign was perhaps not seeking particularly to support or degrade IS, but rather to sell unrelated services, possibly targeting potential buyers in Tunisia. The irrelevant spam frequently referenced sex, with hashtags such as #sex_films and more than 3,000 tweets that all read, "Watch what this young man did with a young woman inside the elevator." One of these provocative sets of tweets did relate to IS: "Watch the scandal of Daesh with women in Ramadan," implying that ISIS members were violating the religious rules of Ramadan.

The Tunisian community shown in Figure C.8 represents 34,899 users who are over-whelmingly anti-ISIS (81 percent regularly use *Daesh*, and only 2 percent use *Islamic State*). The network structure is interesting in that it is far more sparse than the other communities we examined, with comparatively fewer connections between core users and a very sparse periph-ery with many Twitter mentions chains. Coordinating messaging efforts in such a network could prove difficult, due to this unique structure.

Yemen

Talk in this community (see Figure C.9) largely supported IS and criticized the Saudi opera-tion in Yemen as collusion with Western and Shia powers. However, this assessment was com-plicated by the significant presence of spam-like activity.

Conspicuously present phrases such as #automatic_retweet and *retweet, choose one of the following packages* suggested a service selling retweets. Many IS-related hashtags were hijacked and came in long chains of unrelated hashtags, such as #Good_morning and #Savio_Cup, an Indian basketball tournament.

One resonant message was the idea of exposing the true nature of IS, with tweets such as "Your eyes are lying about the Islamic State, #The_people_rule," and "mislead you about Daesh." Pro-IS messages dominated, with hashtags such as #I_spread_the_accounts_of_the_supporters, and #news_of_the_caliphate. This hashtag was also likely in support of IS: #Islamic_State_claims_the_Texas_operation. Mentions of the pro-IS media outlet #A'maq_Agency were also overpresent. However, other tweets opposed IS. One overpresent anti-IS hashtag read: #the_Daeshis_have_attributes_of_the_Khawarij, a reference to a splinter move-ment in the early Islamic period whose members rejected the authority of any ruler who

Figure C.9
Yemeni Community Active Users (per Day)

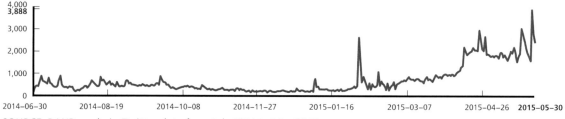

SOURCE: RAND analysis, Twitter data from July 2014 to May 2015.
RAND *RR1328-C.9*

deviated from their interpretation of Islam. Another declared, #The_Islamic_State_liberates_ destroys_and_imprisons. Support for Syrian rebels more generally also featured prominently, with conspicuous mentions of Jaysh al-Islam and Jaysh al-Fatih, as well as the popular hashtag #kill_Bashar_al-Asad.

Another resonant message was criticism of the Saudi operation in Yemen as secretly against ISIS and the people of Yemen, and in the interests of the West. Overpresent terms included *Yemen* and #End_Operation_Decisive_Storm. More than 200 of these tweets said, "The King Salman [King of Saudi Arabia] interferes in Yemen to prevent the rush of people to the bosom of the #Islamic_State." Another hundred read, "O People of Yemen, wisdom and rally around #the_Islamic_State and do not imagine that the Crusaders are acting in your interest." Other popular phrases and hashtags referenced Saudi Arabia and the Gulf more generally, such as

Figure C.10
Yemeni Community Network Representation

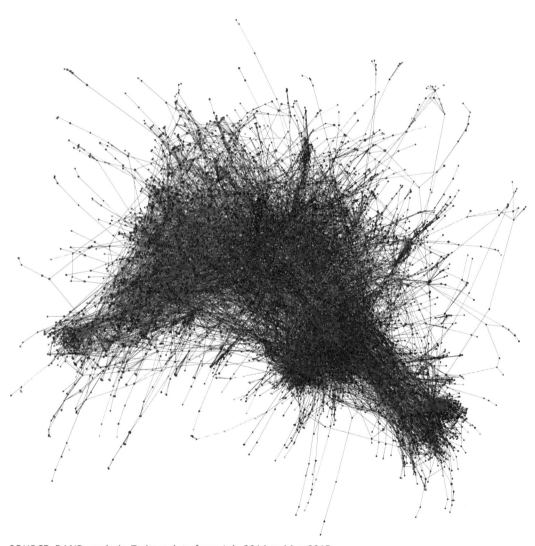

SOURCE: RAND analysis, Twitter data from July 2014 to May 2015.
NOTE: Node size indicates in-degree; color indicates stance (blue = anti-ISIS, red = pro-ISIS, green = both, gray = neither), as determined by use of *Daesh* versus *Islamic State*.
RAND *RR1328-C.10*

#Hey_Saudis, *Saudi Emergency Forces*, and *Arabs and Gulfis and foreigners*. Another tweet alleged, "Saudi Arabia supports the *Rawafidh* [derogatory term for Shia]."

Anti-Shiism and anti-Iranianism accompanied discussion of Iraq, with overpresent negative references to *the Iranians*, #Popular_Mobilization_Front (PMF, *al-Hashd_al-Sha'bi*), and *Rawafidh*, a derogatory term for Shia. *The Awakenings* (Sahwat, anti-IS Sunni groups) were also criticized heavily. Not all such tweets supported IS. One read, ". . . the Jews . . . the *Rawafidh* . . . Daesh, all of them in the same bloody mud stained with blood," and another said, "Daesh is an Iranian creation."

The Yemeni community–mentions network shown in Figure C.10 has a markedly different structure than that of the other Sunni communities we examined. While the Egyptian and Saudi communities have the possibility of being split along anti- and pro-ISIS lines, the Yemeni community is sharply divided between them (48 percent use *Daesh* regularly, 31 percent *Islamic State*). It also appears that most of the potentially neutral accounts (those that use *Daesh* and *Islamic State* approximately equally, 9 percent of this community) are generally within the pro-ISIS user group, though further analysis would be needed to validate that conclusion. To find potential influencers within this community, it will be important to identify which accounts bridge both groups and which are prominent within their respective groups— essentially repeating some of the analysis in this report, but at a finer-grained level.

Jordan

Jordanians—particularly those decrying the death of Moath al-Kasabeh, the Jordanian pilot burned alive on February 3, 2015—dominated this community (see Figure C.11). This coincided with surges in nationalism and support for Jordanian participation in the air campaign against IS.

The Jordanian identity of this community was evidenced by the extreme overpresence of the words *Jordan*, *Jordanian*, and *Jordanians*. Not all opposition to ISIS was directly linked to the Jordanian pilot; popular phrases included #stamp_on_Daesh, #a_cry_from_Raqqa, #Daesh_is_a_creation_of_Iran_and_Russia, and *the war against Daesh*. References to ISIS members were *dogs of Daesh, dogs of fire, may God curse [them]*.

However, talk in this community was dominated by outrage over the death of the Jordanian pilot burned alive by IS; this shock fueled a desire for vengeance and translated to strong support for the Jordanian Air Force. The pilot's name, Moath al-Kasabeh, was repeated

Figure C.11
Jordanian Community Active Users (per Day)

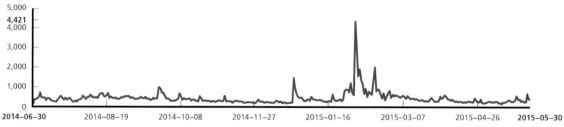

SOURCE: RAND analysis, Twitter data from July 2014 to May 2015.
NOTE: The y-axis ranges from 0 to 4,421 tweets per day.
RAND *RR1328-C.11*

over and over. Highly overpresent terms and hashtags included *the martyr*, *the pilot*, #We_are_all_Moath, #Moath_true_martyr, #Moath_al-Kasabeh, and #Daesh_burns_the_Jordanian_pilot. Calls for vengeance came in the form of popular hashtags such as #we_revenge_ourselves_against_Daesh and #the_next_Jordanian_response. These hashtags accompanied many messages of support for the *Royal Air Force*.

This outrage translated into support for Jordanian participation in the international coalition against IS. For instance, one tweet read, "It is a universal obligation [*wajib 'alimi*, mandatory duty in Islam], and should be the first of the obligations, the forces of the international coalition against the Daesh Terrorist Organization." Another tweet referenced ISIS's use of fire to kill, which is against Islamic prohibitions on war: "May God support them against the wicked, bomb the criminals, if the coalition burns, in the same way to destroy Daesh completely." Another user identified himself firmly as with the campaign by using *we*, the first-person pronoun: "And we killed seven thousand terrorists since the start of the strikes in cooperation with the international coalition." This sense of taking ownership of the war against ISIS was supported by the conspicuous use of the phrase *our war*.

Figure C.12
Jordanian Community Network Representation

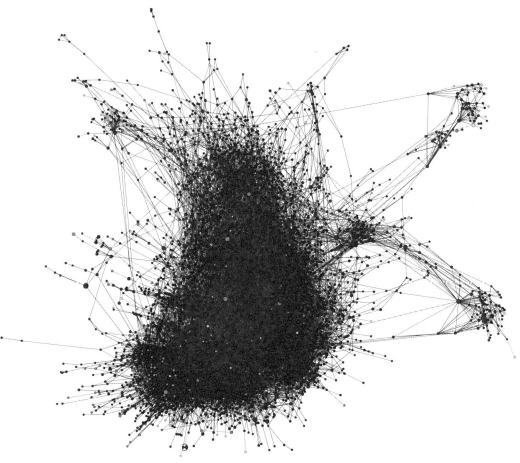

SOURCE: RAND analysis, Twitter data from July 2014 to May 2015.
NOTE: Node size indicates in-degree; color indicates stance (blue = anti-ISIS, red = pro-ISIS, green = both, gray = neither), as determined by use of *Daesh* versus *Islamic State*.
RAND *RR1328-C.12*

The Jordanian community shown in Figure C.12 represents 13,381 users, most of whom are anti-ISIS (81 percent use *Daesh*, 5 percent *Islamic State*). As we have seen with some of the other communities, the few ISIS supporters and those who might be neutral (only 4 percent in this community) generally form a pocket within the network (lower left in the network diagram). This network also has a few outlying structures that could be further characterized using lexical analysis.

Libya

This community (see Figure C.13) appeared to consist mostly of Libyans, along with perhaps some Tunisians. These users seemed to oppose ISIS as well as all other organizations and leaders mentioned, with many allegations of behind-the-scenes collusion between Libyan politicians, militant groups, and the West.

This community's primarily Libyan identity was clear from the conspicuous overpresence of *Libya*, *Libyans*, *the Libyan*, as well as the names of Libyan cities and towns: Sirte, Nofaliya, Benghazi, Al-Sabri, Derna, Tripoli, Misrata, Laithi, Ajdabiya. Names repeated over and over included Khalifa Haftar, the commander of the internationally backed Libyan government, Omar al-Hassi, Libyan politician who was prime minister under the Tripoli-based General National Congress until March 2015, and Muamar Qaddafi, former Libyan ruler. The Libyan army and Libyan Dawn (*Fajr Libya*), a group of Libyan-conflict participants that includes the Muslim Brotherhood, featured prominently, as did "Operation Dignity," the name of General Haftar's push to retake Benghazi. Mentions of *Tunisia* and *the Tunisian* were also overpresent. Entities from the Gulf whose names were repeated frequently included Qatari cleric Hassan Hamoud and UAE-based Sky News (Sky News Arabia, undated).

The themes prevalent among members of this community painted a grim picture of violence and confusion. The words *revolutionaries*, *battalion*, and *the blood* were conspicuously present. Most tweets about Ansar al-Sharia, the Libyan branch of the extremist organization allied with al-Qa'ida in the Islamic Maghreb, were negative, as were most tweets about the ISIS attack on the Corinthia Hotel in January 2015 and most tweets about General Haftar. One tweet read, "For whoever has lost the objectivity to confront General Haftar since August 8, 2014, the coalition aircraft launched 7,000 raids." Another said, "This massacre was not committed by Daesh in Anbar, but rather by Haftar's militias in Benghazi, the victims were a doctor and four nurses, accused of treating the rebels." As an example of the complicated web of

Figure C.13
Libyan Community Active Users (per Day)

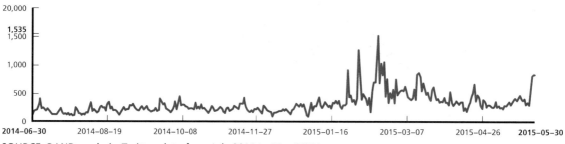

SOURCE: RAND analysis, Twitter data from July 2014 to May 2015.

associations spun in this community, one tweet advised: "Try to understand, Haftar says that he is fighting Daesh and the Tripoli government, while Haftar is an ally of bloody Qaddafi, the last one who praises Daesh, and the government of Tripoli." More comprehensibly, another

Figure C.14
Libyan Community Network Representation

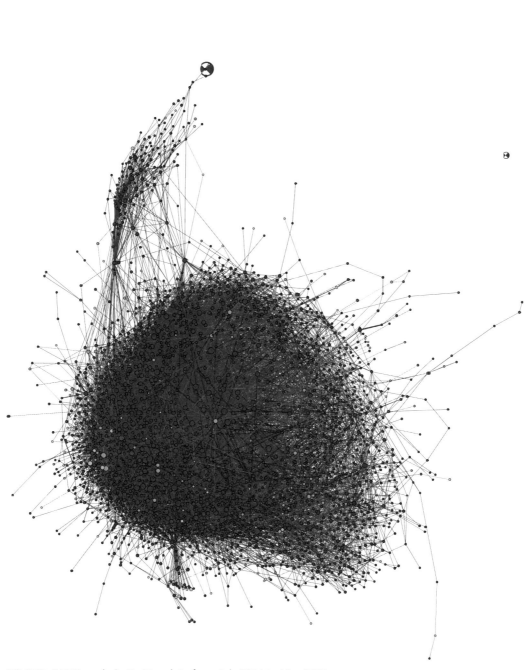

SOURCE: RAND analysis, Twitter data from July 2014 to May 2015.
NOTE: Node size indicates in-degree; color indicates stance (blue = anti-ISIS, red = pro-ISIS, green = both, gray = neither), as determined by use of *Daesh* versus *Islamic State*.
RAND *RR1328-C.14*

tweet read, "The important thing is, Haftar is evil." One popular hashtag was #Ambassador_Mark_Grant_UN_delegation; Mark Grant was the UK ambassador to the United Nations until 2015. One tweet that used this hashtag explained, "The British ambassador confirmed to the world that Daesh was created and is supported by Western intelligence agencies."

The Libyan community shown in Figure C.14 is the smallest we analyzed, with 8,298 users, of which 78 percent regularly used the term *Daesh* and 7 percent used the term *Islamic State* when referencing ISIS. As with the GCC community, this network displays a classic core-periphery structure with the most connected and most mentioned users forming a strong core and other, potentially less influential accounts on the periphery. However, there is one unique structural feature—a cluster of users strongly connected to each other and connected to the majority of the network through two main accounts (outlying structure at top left of the figure). Lexical analysis could be used to reveal what makes this cluster different from the rest of the community but was beyond the scope of this project.

References

Arab Opinion Project, "The Military Campaign Against the Islamic State in Iraq and the Levant: Arab Public Opinion," Arab Center for Research and Policy Studies, November 11, 2014.

Berger, J. M., and Jonathon Morgan, "The ISIS Twitter Census: Defining and Describing the Population of ISIS Supporters on Twitter," Brookings Institution, No. 20, March 2015.

Borgatti, Stephen P., Martin G. Everett, and Jeffrey P. Johnson, *Analyzing Social Networks*, Thousand Oaks, Calif.: SAGE Publications Ltd., 2013.

Carter, Joseph, Shiraz Maher, and Peter Neumann, "#Greenbirds: Measuring Importance and Influence in Syrian Foreign Fighter Networks," London: International Centre for the Study of Radicalization and Political Violence, 2014.

Clauset, Aaron, M. Newman, and C. Moore, "Finding Community Structure in Very Large Networks," *Physical Review E*, Vol. 70, No. 6, 2004.

Easley, David, and Jon Kleinberg, *Networks, Crowds and Markets: Reasoning About a Highly Connected World*, Cambridge, UK: Cambridge University Press, 2010.

Freeman, Linton, "A Set of Measures of Centrality Based on Betweenness," *Sociometry*, Vol. 40, 1977, pp. 35–41.

———, *The Development of Social Network Analysis*, Vancouver: Empirical Press, 2004.

Hall, John, "Twitter Suspends 10,000 Accounts Linked to ISIS in Just 24 Hours 'for Tweeting Violent Threats'" *Daily Mail*, April 10, 2015. As of April 12, 2016: http://www.dailymail.co.uk/news/article-3033600/Twitter-suspends-10-000-accounts-linked-ISIS-just-24-hours-tweeting-violent-threats.html

Hanneman, Robert, and Mark Riddle, *Introduction to Social Network Methods*, Riverside, Calif.: University of California, 2005. As of May 30, 2013: http://faculty.ucr.edu/~hanneman/

Hardy, Donald, *The Body in Flannery O'Connor's Fiction: Computational Technique and Linguistic Voice*, Columbia, S.C.: University of South Carolina Press, 2007.

Helmus, Todd C., Erin York, and Peter Chalk, *Promoting Online Voices for Countering Violent Extremism*, Santa Monica, Calif.: RAND Corporation, RR-130-OSD, 2013. As of July 11, 2016: http://www.rand.org/pubs/research_reports/RR130.html

"Isis, Isil or Da'ish? What to Call Militants in Iraq," BBC News, June 24, 2014.

Jackson, Matthew, *Social and Economic Networks*, Princeton, N.J.: Princeton University Press, 2010.

Kenny, Dorothy, *Lexis and Creativity in Translation: A Corpus Based Approach*, London: Routledge, 2014.

Leskovec, Jure, "SNAP: Stanford Network Analysis Project," Stanford, Calif.: Stanford University, 2014.

Magdy, Alid, Kareem Darwish, and Ignmar Weber, "#FailedRevolutions: Using Twitter to Study the Antecedents of ISIS Support," Doha, Qatar: Qatar Computing Research Institute, Qatar Foundation, March 9, 2015.

Momin, M. Malik, Hemank Lamba, Constantine Nakos, and Jurgen Pfeffer, "Population Bias in Geotagged Tweets," *Papers from the 2015 ICWSM Workshop on Standards and Practices in Large-Scale Social Media Research*, Oxford, UK, May 16, 2015, pp 18–27.

Miller, Greg, "Panel Casts Doubt on U.S. Propaganda Efforts Against ISIS," *Washington Post*, December 2, 2015. As of April 12, 2016:
https://www.washingtonpost.com/world/national-security/panel-casts-doubt-on-us-propaganda-efforts-against-isis/2015/12/02/ab7f9a14-9851-11e5-94f0-9eeaff906ef3_story.html

Newman, Mark, *Networks: An Introduction*, Oxford, UK: Oxford University Press, 2010.

Norton-Taylor, Richard, "Up to 30,000 Foreign Fighters Have Gone to Syria and Iraq Since 2011—Report," *Guardian*, November 17, 2015.

Paquette, Danielle, "Why Young American Women Are Joining ISIS," *Washington Post*, November 17, 2015.

Phillips, Robbin, Greg Cordel, Geno Church, and Spike Jones, *Brains on Fire: Igniting Powerful, Sustainable, Word of Mouth Movements*, Wiley, August 31, 2010.

Pollock, David, "ISIS Has Almost No Popular Support in Egypt, Saudi Arabia, or Lebanon," Washington, D.C.: The Washington Institute for Near East Policy, October 14, 2015.

Rand, Paul, *Highly Recommended: Harnessing the Power of Word of Mouth and Social Media to Build Your Brand and Your Business*, New York: McGraw-Hill Education, September 20, 2013.

Rayson, Paul, and Roger Garside, "Comparing Corpora Using Frequency Profiling," in *Proceedings of the Workshop on Comparing Corpora,* Vol. 9, Association for Computational Linguistics, October 2002.

Scott, John, *Social Network Analysis: A Handbook*, 2nd Edition, Thousand Oaks, Calif.: SAGE Publications Ltd., 2000.

Scott, Mike, *WordSmith Tools*, Oxford, UK: Oxford University Press, 1996.

———, "Mapping Key Words to Problem and Solution," in *Patterns of Text: In Honour of Michael Hoey*, Amsterdam: Benjamins, 2001.

Sky News Arabia, Arabic home page, undated. As of April 12, 2016:
http://www.skynewsarabia.com/web/home

"This Is the Promise of Allah," speech by Abu Muhammad al-'Adnani, English translation by al-Hayat Media Center, June 29, 2014.

"Transforming Education in the Arab World," *Arab Social Media Report*, Dubai School of Government, June 2013. As of April 12, 2016:
http://www.arabsocialmediareport.com/UserManagement/PDF/ASMR_5_Report_Final.pdf

"Twitter in the Arab Region," *Arab Social Media Report*, Dubai School of Government, undated. As of May 30, 2013:
http://www.arabsocialmediareport.com/Twitter/LineChart.aspx?&PriMenuID=18&CatID=25&mnu=Cat

Voices from the Blogs, "ISIS: Perception on News On-Line and Social Media Considering Only Posts and Articles Written in Arabic Language," report produced for *Guardian*, November 28, 2014.

Walker, Rob, "The Marketing of No Marketing," *International New York Times*, June 22, 2003. As of April 12, 2016:
http://www.nytimes.com/2003/06/22/magazine/the-marketing-of-no-marketing.html?pagewanted=all

Wasserman, Stanley, and Katherine Faust, *Social Network Analysis: Methods and Applications*, Cambridge, UK: Cambridge University Press, 1994.

Winter, Charlie, *The Virtual "Caliphate": Understanding Islamic State's Propaganda Strategy*, London: Quilliam Foundation, July 2015. As of April 12, 2016:
https://www.quilliamfoundation.org/wp/wp-content/uploads/publications/free/the-virtual-caliphate-understanding-islamic-states-propaganda-strategy.pdf

Wright, Ted, *Fizz: Harness the Power of Word of Mouth Marketing to Drive Brand Growth*, New York: McGraw-Hill Education, November 11, 2014.

Yourish, Karen, Derek Watkins, and Tom Giratikanon, "Where ISIS Has Directed and Inspired Attacks Around the World," *New York Times*, March 22, 2016. As of April 12, 2016:
http://www.nytimes.com/interactive/2015/06/17/world/middleeast/map-isis-attacks-around-the-world.html?_r=0